THE MYTHOLOGY
AZTEC & M

THE MYTHOLOGY OF THE
AZTEC & MAYA

An illustrated encyclopedia of the gods, myths and legends of
the Aztecs, Maya and other peoples of ancient Mexico and central
America, with over 240 fine art illustrations and photographs

CHARLES PHILLIPS · CONSULTANT: DR DAVID M JONES

southwater

This edition is published by Southwater

Southwater is an imprint of Anness Publishing Ltd
Hermes House, 88–89 Blackfriars Road, London SE1 8HA
tel. 020 7401 2077; fax 020 7633 9499
www.southwaterbooks.com; info@anness.com

© Anness Publishing Ltd 2006

UK agent: The Manning Partnership Ltd, 6 The Old Dairy, Melcombe Road, Bath BA2 3LR;
tel. 01225 478444; fax 01225 478440; sales@manning-partnership.co.uk

UK distributor: Grantham Book Services Ltd, Isaac Newton Way,
Alma Park Industrial Estate, Grantham, Lincs NG31 9SD; tel. 01476 541080;
fax 01476 541061; orders@gbs.tbs-ltd.co.uk

North American agent/distributor: National Book Network, 4501 Forbes Boulevard,
Suite 200, Lanham, MD 20706; tel. 301 459 3366; fax 301 429 5746;
www.nbnbooks.com

Australian agent/distributor: Pan Macmillan Australia, Level 18, St Martins Tower,
31 Market St, Sydney, NSW 2000; tel. 1300 135 113; fax 1300 135 103;
customer.service@macmillan.com.au

New Zealand agent/distributor: David Bateman Ltd, 30 Tarndale Grove, Off Bush Road,
Albany, Auckland; tel. (09) 415 7664; fax (09) 415 8892

Publisher: Joanna Lorenz
Editorial Director: Helen Sudell
Editor: Joy Wotton
Designer: Nigel Partridge
Maps: Peter Bull Art Studio
Illustrations: Vanessa Card
Production Controller: Claire Rae
Editorial Reader: Jay Thundercliffe

Previously published as part of a larger volume,
The Illustrated Encyclopedia of Aztec & Maya

1 3 5 7 9 10 8 6 4 2

CONTENTS

INTRODUCTION

The peoples of Mesoamerica entered into an intense relationship with the natural world and with the gods and goddesses who lived in it and sustained natural forms. They saw a world filled with at times dangerous sacred power that demanded ritual worship; they believed this power could take shape in a vast range of deities who shifted between human, animal or symbolic forms as need or desire dictated. Mesoamericans also had an enduring connection across time: they passed stories about deities, religious practices and sacred narratives from culture to culture. To Mesoamericans these stories would have been history.

Local practice before the Conquest meant that much of Mesoamerican mythology and history was transmitted orally from generation to generation and never written down. Weather and land conditions often did not favour the survival of early remains. But the major part of the blame for the paucity of surviving remains must be shouldered by the Spanish conquerors themselves. After they had captured Tenochtitlán in 1521, they vandalized the city, breaking images of the gods, melting down treasures into ingots to be sent back to Europe, tearing down buildings and using the materials for the foundations of their colony, New Spain.

This survey of the 'mythologized' narratives of Mesoamerica covers creation tales, accounts of earth and sky, narratives of the gods and goddesses, stories associated with fertility and harvest and imaginings of the afterlife. This section concludes with an investigation of how myth-like accounts and historical fact were blended in Mesoamericans' narratives of past achievements and even in their accounts of defeat at the hands of the Spanish conquistadors.

Left: The imposing Pyramid of the Moon, in Teotihuacán, contains a hidden burial chamber with a sacrificial victim.

AZTEC HISTORY AND MYTHOLOGY

Most of the written evidence we have of Aztec customs, beliefs, history and mythology was recorded after the Conquest, in manuscript books or codices written by young natives educated in Spanish schools and in reports written by the Spanish chroniclers, based on what they saw and heard from locals.

WRITTEN SOURCES

An important example is the *Codex Mendoza*, commissioned *c.*1525 by the first Spanish Viceroy, Don Antonio de Mendoza. It contains an account of the growth of the Aztec empire illustrated and written by native Mesoamericans based on older pictorial records.

The movements of the México/Aztec and other tribal groups prior to the establishment of Tenochtitlán are described in 16th-century manuscripts such as the *Codex Aubin* and the *Codex Xólotl* and also in the 17th-century history recorded by Fernando de Alva Ixtlilxóchitl. All were based on oral histories and earlier codices, now lost.

Among the Spanish chroniclers' accounts is Friar Bernardino de Sahagún's compendious 12-volume *General History of the Things of New Spain*, completed in 1569. His fellow Churchman Diego Durán compiled both the *History of the Indies of New Spain* and the *Book of the Gods and Rites and the Ancient Calendar*. First-hand accounts of the Conquest itself survive in the letters written by Hernán Cortés to Charles V and in *True History of the Conquest of New Spain*, written by Bernal Díaz del Castillo, a member of Cortés' force.

Above: Serpents writhe round the neck of the Aztec earth goddess Coatlícue. Ritual victims were decapitated in her honour.

REWRITING THE PAST

Scholars treat all the surviving written evidence with caution as many accounts blend history and mythology in a dense combination that is difficult to interpret, not least because it is full of repetitions and contradictions. A good example is that of the Aztecs' treatment of Tula, which combines knowledge handed down by oral tradition of the historical city (flourished *c.*AD950–1150) with the myth of Tollán ('the Place of the Reeds'), home to wondrous craftsmen, where the god Quetzalcóatl ruled in the guise of the prince Topiltzin. In general, Mesoamerican peoples looked to the past for justification of the present.

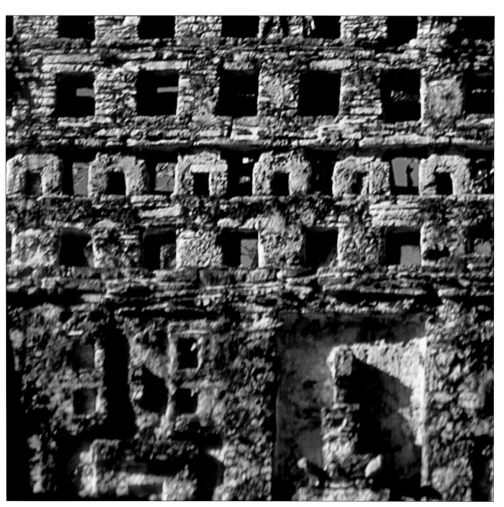

Left: The Palace of King Yaxchilán contains a sculpture honouring the 8th-century AD Maya monarch Bird Jaguar.

Above: Aztec codices are more numerous than their Maya counterparts. The Codex Magliabechano *is a late 1500s copy of a pre-Hispanic manuscript. It contains valuable information on Aztec worship and the use of the ritual calendar.*

The Aztecs, for example, rewrote their own history to establish that their destiny was to dominate other peoples and expand their own territories. The Aztecs often presented events or themes that were common to many cultures as unique

'historical' happenings. The Aztecs claimed they found their origin in the 'Place of the Seven Caves', but this origin story was common to the beliefs of many Mesoamerican groups.

Yet the Mesoamericans themselves viewed these accounts as history, even though the narratives contain non-sequential episodes and metaphorical accounts of events. Because of the Mesoamericans' willingness to blend fact with what the modern mind would class as myth in historical accounts, we know nothing for certain of events that took place more than 400 years before the Conquest. All scholars can do in the circumstances is to gauge the meaning of surviving buildings and ruins in the light of the latest knowledge.

Left: Mesoamerican societies had an enduring fascination with the jaguar. This clay model was made by an Aztec artist.

STELAE

Many carved inscriptions survive in Maya lands, notably on stelae, stone columns set up during the Classic Period in the 3rd to 9th centuries AD. They bear portraits of the 'holy kings' of Maya city-states and commemorate the rulers' accessions and jubilees, battle victories and important religious sacrifices, which sometimes included the humiliation and slaughter of a rival king.

One stela, erected in honour of King Cauac Sky in Quiriguá, south-eastern Guatemala, is 10m (33ft) tall and weighs 10 tons. It was set up in AD771. The Maya stopped erecting carved stelae in the 9th century AD and scholars believe that after this point they probably kept their records in books. The books were destroyed by the Spanish, but the stelae survive, providing an invaluable source of information about Maya history and culture in the Classic Period.

UNLOCKING THE SECRETS OF MAYA SOCIETY

In the mid-20th century, a breakthrough in the interpretation of Maya hieroglyphs led to a major reappraisal of the very nature of Maya society. Earlier scholars thought that the hieroglyphs combined a picture-image (rebus) and a symbol representing a word or idea (logogram). But in 1952 Soviet language specialist Yuri Knorosov showed that Maya hieroglyphs were also phonetic: different signs represented combinations of vowels and consonants and were used to spell out words. Phonetic signs, he argued, were written or carved alongside logograms. Maya experts resisted Knorosov's theory for some years , but in time they came to realize that he was right. Now they could begin to read the inscriptions, with results that helped to turn our understanding of the Maya on its head.

NEW UNDERSTANDINGS
In the early 20th century, scholars had recognized that the inscriptions contained a great deal of information about the ritual calendar and astronomy. They thought the carvings on the stelae were of priests rather than kings, and that

Above: The Chiapas rainforest crowds in on the ruins at Bonampak of the court of Lord Chan Muan, who reigned AD776–795.

images of beheaded victims represented sacred rites. They argued that the Maya were a peaceful people led by priestly astronomers. However, later scholars who could read the writing began to see that the inscriptions were about events in a king's reign. They understood that the carvings were of kings and that the sacrificial victims were often rival kings put to ritual death after defeat. A new, more accurate image emerged of the Maya as a martial people living in city-states that were almost constantly at war.

Another major breakthrough in our understanding of the Maya also occurred in 1952, with the discovery of a great royal tomb beneath a mortuary monument in the Maya city of Palenque. Mexican architect Alberto Ruz Lhuillier was excavating the vast Temple of Inscriptions there when his curiosity was aroused by one of the slabs on the temple floor. This particular stone slab was cut with a double row of holes that could, he conjectured, be used as finger grips to raise the stone. When he had the stone

lifted, he discovered a narrow stairway leading downward. The stairway had been deliberately blocked with rubble, which Lhuillier painstakingly cleared over the following four years. In June 1952 he discovered the stairs led to a chamber, beyond which he found a great funerary crypt 9m long and 7m in height (30ft by 23ft). The crypt held a carved stone sarcophagus in which lay a body later identified from inscriptions as that of King Pacal, ruler of Palenque in the 7th–8th centuries AD. Prior to Lhuillier's breakthrough, scholars had generally understood that the Maya built stepped pyramids as temples, but the discovery of Pacal in his magnificent royal tomb suggested that some of the pyramids were erected primarily as funerary monuments to honour deceased monarchs.

'PAINTED WALLS'
Six years earlier, in 1946, an American photographer called Giles Healey made another remarkable discovery deep in the rainforest of the Mexican state of Chiapas. Healey, who was searching for Maya ruins in the area, was led by locals to a city they referred to as Bonampak ('Painted Walls'). There he found a three-roomed building

---

ARCHAEOLOGIST AND LITERARY SLEUTH
Mexican archaeologist Alfonso Caso y Andrade (1896–1970) bridged the gap between the interpreters of ancient literature and the investigators of ruined sites. Not only did Andrade decipher a number of Mixtec codices in the course of his work, he also performed a painstaking archaeological study at Monte Albán, establishing a chronology for the occupation of the site in the Oaxaca valley and demonstrating that the Mixtec people occupied Monte Albán in the wake of the Zapotecs. Andrade published the celebrated *El Mapa de Teozacaoalco* in 1949 and *Kings and Kingdoms of the Mixteca* in 1970.

Above: The murals at Bonampak depict court life and celebrations marking a battle won by Lord Chan Muan in AD790.

whose walls were decorated with a remarkable series of murals that contain vivid images of life at a Maya royal court in the 8th century AD, including royal accessions, battles, musical performances and other ceremonies. In recent years, scholars have used digital technology to enhance photographs of the images and restore their original bright colours. The natives' name stuck: the city, about 30km (18 miles) from Yaxchilán, became known as Bonampak.

Archaeological work on Tenochtitlán was complicated by the fact that the capital of the Spanish colony of New Spain and later the vast metropolis of Mexico City were built on top of Aztec ruins. Important discoveries were made in the course of building work. In 1790, workers laying flagstones in the main square of Mexico City discovered the 24-ton Sun Stone, which commemorates the five Aztecs 'suns' or ages, together with a remarkable sculpture of Coatlícue, the earth goddess. A carving of the earth lord Tlaltecuhtli was found in 1968 during digging for a metro line. In 1978, an electrical company worker uncovered part of a 3.25m- (10ft 9in) diameter monolith depicting the dismembered goddess Coyolxauhqui, who in myth was killed by her brother Huitzilopochtli. Scholars knew that the foundations of the Aztecs' Great Pyramid were adjacent to the spot where the monolith was found. The discovery of what became known as the 'Coyolxauhqui Stone' resulted in a major excavation of the foundations of the Great Pyramid over the following years.

Archaeologists' investigations brought many valuable insights into Teotihuacán, the site in the north-east Valley of Mexico that was revered by the Aztecs as the 'place of the gods'. The city was surveyed systematically in the 1960s and 1970s by American archaeologist René Millon. One of the major breakthroughs came by accident. In 1971, digging during preparations for a *son et lumière* ('sound and light') show uncovered a cave in volcanic lava beneath the city's most sacred building, the vast Pyramid of the Sun. Offerings found there have been dated to many centuries before the Pyramid was built in the 2nd century AD, suggesting that the city had been built on an ancient site of pilgrimage. The Aztecs frequently visited ruined sites such as Teotihuacán, sometimes taking artefacts from the site and sometimes adding others of a different period.

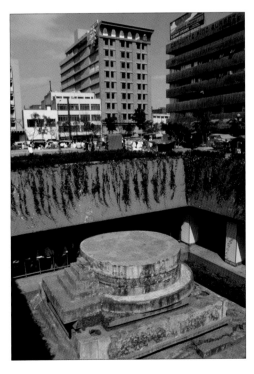

Right: In Mexico City the Aztec past is never far away. A subway station is home to a temple honouring the wind god Éhecatl.

CHAPTER ONE

CREATION AND THE FIRST PEOPLES

The Aztecs understood both time and space in terms of four cardinal directions and a central anchoring point. They believed that the Great Pyramid in Tenochtitlán was the centre of the Earth, which spread in a vast flat expanse to east and west and north and south. Four gods and their directions were also associated with the four 'suns' or ages that had preceded the current era on Earth. The first age was associated with Tezcatlipoca and with the north. The second was under the control of Quetzalcóatl, and linked to the west, while the third was governed by the rain god Tláloc and connected to the south. The fourth age was presided over by Tláloc's consort Chalchiúhtlicue and connected to the east. The fifth 'sun' or contemporary age was linked to the centre because the number of the centre is five; it was under the control of the fire god Xiuhtecuhtli.

According to Aztec cosmology, above the flat Earth rose thirteen layers of heaven, where Ometeotl, the supreme creator, dwelt. Beneath the earth were nine levels of the underworld or Mictlán, presided over by Mictlantecuhtli, god of that realm, with his consort Mictecacíhuatl. In some accounts, waters encircled the Earth at the farthest reaches of north, south, east and west and curved up above the land to make the sky. If the gods decreed, the sky waters could fall to wipe out men and all their achievements in one cataclysmic flood.

Left: An illustration from the Mixtec-Aztec Codex Fejérváry-Mayer *depicts the fire god Xiuhtecuhtli at the centre of the universe with four directions emanating outwards.*

THE POWER IN THE CENTRE: COSMOLOGY

At north, south, east and west of the Mesoamerican universe stood four pillars, or trees, that both supported and connected the three levels of the cosmos. In the centre was a fifth tree, whose roots were in the underworld but whose topmost branches touched the very highest of the celestial planes. The four other trees at the points of the compass were in fact outgrowths of the main cosmic tree. The trees stood on hollow hills and were themselves hollow, and within them the power of the underworld and of the heavens was always flowing, powering the repeating movements of time, of the seasons, of the sun, moon, stars and planets and of the energy recycled in acts of blood sacrifice. Only after the creation of the four trees of north, south, east and west could time be measured and sacred events honoured through use of the ritual calendar.

THE FOUR GODS

In one Aztec myth, four gods were born, sometimes known as the four Tezcatlipocas after the god of night and destiny, the sons of the supreme creator Ometeotl in his dual male-female forms Ometecuhtli and Omecíhuatl. According to this tradition, all was chaos in the first days until the four sons agreed to separate heaven and earth and take the form of the four world trees at the four cardinal points. Their act of separation created a space in which the new world could be made.

Right: This stela, carved in c.1250, shows the Earth Monster Tlaltecuhtli, ravenous for human heart blood.

A developed iconography was associated with these myths. Each of the four points of the compass was associated with a god, a glyph, at least one colour and a plant. For example, the glyph for north – the direction of Tezcatlipoca – represented a *técpatl*, the knife used for sacrificing victims; its colours were yellow and black. North was associated with the xerophyte tree, which naturally grew in northern regions of Mesoamerica. Death and cold were linked to the region, which was known as Mictlampa (the land of death). Dampness was associated with the south, where Huitzilopochtli held sway. The glyph for south represented the rabbit; the region was linked to the colour blue. The west was governed by Quetzalcóatl. Its glyph represented a house and its colour was white. The east was associated with Xipe Totec and its glyph showed a reed. Its colour was red.

Sometimes the Aztecs likened the Earth to a flower with four petals, one for each quadrant. One interpretation of the myth of the four suns or ages is that in each successive age one of the four quadrants and its tree or pillar was created and that in the fifth (current) age, the centre – that is, the Templo Mayor at the Great Pyramid in Tenochtitlán – came into being.

THE WORLD TREE

This basic cosmology was common in Mesoamerica. The Maya also told of a vast flat earth, with thirteen levels of heaven rising above and nine layers of underworld beneath. The Quiché Maya told in the *Popol Vuh* how, in the first hours of

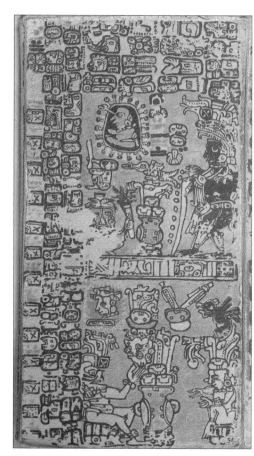

Above: A Maya priest ceremonially plants corn. Maintaining the Earth's fertility was a focus of Mesoamerican religious life.

creation, the earth and sky emerged following a 'fourfold cornering [and] measuring', a process analogous to the one used by Maya farmers to plot their fields. The Maya also understood that in each of the four corners of creation grew a tree, supporting the sky in that place, and that in the centre rose a greater world tree, which connected the realms of earth, heaven and the underworld. The Maya king Pacal, ruler of Palenque, is depicted on the lid of his magnificent sarcophagus travelling down to the underworld along the trunk of this great cosmic tree.

In some accounts of Maya cosmography, the four supporting structures are not trees but giants called bacabs who, curiously, were patrons of beekeepers. A depiction of the bacabs survives on an 8th–9th

Right: A mural from a residential building in Teotihuacán represents the Earth Mother (centre) supporting a great cosmic tree.

century building at Chichén Itzá that was called the *Iglesia* ('church') by the Spaniards. Their names were Mulac (associated with the north and with white), Kan (linked to the east and yellow), Ix (connected to the west and to black) and Cauac (associated with the south and red). Like the Aztecs, the Maya linked colours to the four directions, but

Below: Xipe Totec (left), god of the east, confronts western deity Quetzalcóatl in an image from the Aztec Codex Borbonicus.

the associations of particular colours was different in the two traditions. For example, white was the colour of the west for the Aztecs but of the north for the Maya. According to the *Books of Chilam Balam*, which contain the legends of the Maya of Yucatán, the four trees at the four corners of the Earth were created in the first moments of each new age.

Below: The ancient rain god worshipped by the Maya as Chac was sometimes said to have power over the cardinal directions.

15

THE MAKING OF THE EARTH

The Mixtec people who made their home in former Zapotec lands in the Oaxaca Valley left a distinctive creation mythology in the images and words of their codices. They told that life began in the union of a nameless couple who lived before time. In the darkness of the unborn world, this pair of gods gave birth to another divine couple named Lord One Deer and Lady One Deer, and they in turn produced many children. Two of Lord and Lady One Deer's offspring pleased their parents by creating a sweet-smelling garden retreat, where flowers bloomed in the gentle shade of magical trees. The first of the Mixtec race climbed from a hole in the trunk of one these remarkable trees. In another account, the Mixtecs were born in a tree that grew in Mexico in Apoala, where a river fed an oasis that

Below: In this Codex Fejérváry-Mayer *image, Tezcatlipoca loses his right foot to the ravening Earth Monster Tlaltecuhtli.*

kept the desert at bay. The men and women went from this place to the four corners of the flat earth, establishing settlements in which to grow crops, raise children and worship the gods. The tree must be a representation of the world tree that Mesoamericans believed linked the spirit realms of the underworld and the many-layered heaven to the earth. It may suggest the family tree of many generations of revered ancestors.

Another version of Mixtec creation mythology told of a primordial era when earth and sky were not separated in complementary opposition as they are now, but were mixed in wetness and darkness. The earth was no more than waterlogged, muddy slime.

Left: This cedar-wood fertility goddess was still receiving offerings when it was discovered in Veracruz in the 19th century.

Then a creator god named Lord Nine Wind arose from the dark and separated the waters from the earth, raising the waters up to form the sky. Mist engulfed the earth, but from the shadowy half-light a divine couple emerged: they were Lord One Deer Jaguar-Serpent and Lady One Deer Jaguar-Serpent. As the sky perfectly complements the earth, so this god and goddess matched one another. They were two separate beings but also at the same time were one divinity encompassing male and female. Their union was fruitful: they created all the other gods of the Mixtec pantheon and built a palace on earth near Apoala. Apoala is well known, but the palace has never been found. It is said that if a mortal man could find this palace, he would discover that on its roof was set a great axe of copper, its blade facing up to and supporting the overarching sky.

CONNECTING STORIES

Lord Nine Wind is a version of the Plumed Serpent god worshipped by the Aztecs as Quetzalcóatl and by the Maya as Kukulcán. In the Quiché Maya creation myth, this same deity is a god of the sea, Sovereign Plumed Serpent, who joins with a sky god to create the unity of sky and earth.

Quetzalcóatl is also a creator-protagonist in the ancient Mexican myth of the Earth Monster Tlaltecuhtli. The Aztecs told the myth, which they had inherited from earlier cultures in the Mexican region, to glorify the gods Quetzalcóatl and Tezcatlipoca. These normally

Above: Ancestors of the Mixtecs depicted in these codex images believed they were born from a tree trunk in a garden paradise.

Earth Monster in his usual form rather than as a serpent and in the course of the great battle lost one of his feet, explaining his one-legged appearance.

The other gods were not pleased to see this violence done to their sister Tlaltecuhtli. Angrily they addressed Quetzalcóatl and Tezcatlipoca, declaring that although she had been torn in pieces, her earthly part would form the basis of future life. They made herbs, flowers and trees grow from her hair, while grasses and sweet-smelling flowers issued from her skin. The life-giving waters of springs and wells were made from her eyes; her mouth made rivers and larger caverns. Her nose gave rise to tall snow-capped mountains and the deep valleys of the sierras where the air is thin. Men and women have grown used to walking on the body of Tlaltecuhtli.

implacable foes decided to join forces to curb Tlaltecuhtli's power when they saw her spreading terror as she walked on the sea. The Earth Monster, like many Mesoamerican deities, was sometimes described as male and sometimes as female; she had a gaping mouth not only on her face but also at her knees, elbows and other joints.

Quetzalcóatl and Tezcatlipoca approached in the form of great, slithering serpents, muscles rippling in their strong shoulders and thighs, their eyes flashing, their long tongues darting from their mouths. Their power was wild as they seized Tlaltecuhtli. One took her left arm and right foot, the other took her right arm and left foot and together they tore her into two great pieces. The first they hurled upwards to make the sky. The second they laid out in four directions to make the flat expanse of the earth. In some accounts Tezcatlipoca fought the

Right: Quetzalcóatl is born from the Earth as Venus the morning star in this carving from a Santa Lucia Cotzumalhuapa stela.

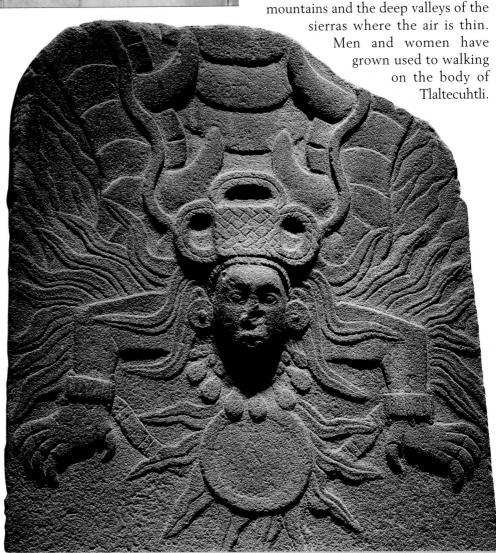

17

ORDER FROM CHAOS: MAYA CREATION STORIES

The Quiché Maya give a detailed account of the creation of the world, and also of the gods' efforts to make the first humans, in their sacred book the *Popol Vuh* ('Book of Advice').

CONVERSATION OF THE GODS

The book tells how the earth was born from the conversation of the gods. Before time began, the waters stretched out endlessly in all directions beneath a blank sky and nothing existed in all the universe except these gathered waters and the sky above. There were no animals or fish, no birds or plants, no rocks and no people. There was not even the potential for life hidden in the waters or the half-darkness of the sky, waiting to be brought to life. Yet the waters did contain the sea god, Gucumatz or 'Sovereign Plumed Serpent', and so despite the near-darkness there was a stirring in the sea, a glittering like blue-green quetzal feathers. His presence was echoed and balanced high above by the sky god Huracán or Heart of Sky.

Huracán came down to meet the sea god and these two divinities, who were deep thinkers and possessed of profound knowledge, started a conversation. Their words brought life into being. The discussion was not easy. They were troubled because they could not at first be sure of the right way to proceed. However, in the course of their debate they created a vision of how life should be in the world, how the trees and bushes should grow and how the people should walk among them. As they talked, it was like the time just before dawn. They discussed how the 'sowing' and the 'dawning' should be brought about. First they decided that the waters should be cleared so that the earth could rise up, and then life could be sown in the earth and in the sky. But they knew that people were needed for this world. The sky and sea gods wanted praise for their work, and they understood that they would not receive this until they created a people capable of keeping track of time and expressing wonder and worship on the appointed days.

The words they used in their discussion had concrete effect. The waters fell away and the earth rose up, just as they said. Mountains appeared and wide forests of pine and cypress trees covered their sides. Waters collected in great lakes and ran on the mountainsides in streams. The gods were pleased. Gucumatz said to Huracán that it was a good thing that the sky god had come down to the sea and

Left: This Classic Maya stone carving represents the Plumed Serpent god feared and worshipped across eras and cultures by Mesoamericans under such names as Quetzalcóatl, Kukulcán and Gucumatz.

Above: Gods above and below – the god depicted on the lower half of this Maya vessel appears to be Chac-Xib-Chac, known for his power to raise hurricanes.

that they had begun their conversation. He had seen from the beginning of their work that it would turn out well. Now they turned to creating animals and people to inhabit the good world.

The *Popol Vuh* account of creation is dense and highly allusive. The scholar and translator of the *Popol Vuh*, Dennis Tedlock, provides many helpful explanations gleaned from his training as a 'daykeeper' or shaman-priest among the contemporary Maya in the region of Momostenango in Guatemala. He states that the 'sowing and dawning' discussed by Huracán and Gucumatz can be understood in terms of the planting and growing of plants, the life cycle of humans and the movements of the planets in the sky. Plant seeds are sown in the earth and 'dawn' by emerging from the ground as

Above: Tezcatlipoca, unpredictable Aztec god, had counterparts among storm deities elsewhere in Mesoamerica.

crops. Similarly, humans are 'sown' in the womb during sexual relations, then 'dawn' nine months later when they emerge screaming into the world. They are also 'sown' in the earth when they are buried after the body's death, but 'dawn' again

as spirits after death, taking the form of celestial lights or stars in the sky. The sun, the moon, Venus and other planets disappear in their own form of 'sowing' when they appear to sink into the earth at the horizon, but they rise again at the appointed time of their dawning.

LORDS OF CREATION

The creator gods are versions of major Mesoamerican deities. Hurakán's name can be understood as 'one-leg' and he is associated with the Classic Period Maya deity Tahil ('Obsidian Mirror' or 'Torch Mirror'), a one-legged god who was honoured in carving at the city of Palenque. Through this connection, Hurakán can be identified with the Aztec god Tezcatlipoca ('Lord of the Smoking Mirror') who, among many attributes, was a divinity of hurricanes, wore an obsidian mirror and was said to be one-legged (in some accounts, because he lost a leg while fighting the Earth Monster Tlaltecuhtli).

Tezcatlipoca was also a god of rains and Huracán's name is linked linguistically with the words used by the Quiché Maya to describe the very large raindrops that come before and after thunderstorms. Sovereign Plumed Serpent or Gucumatz is more obviously a version of the feathered serpent deity Quetzalcóatl, and is also known as Kukulcán by the Yucatec-speaking Maya.

Left: This powerful but simple Maya mask was fashioned from jade to be worn as an ornament on the chest or a belt.

Above: This Classic Maya terracotta vase (c.AD650–950) bears the face of a sky god, perhaps the sun god Ah Kin Chil.

The *Popol Vuh* creation story describes these creator gods both as individuals and as members of a group. The group of sky gods includes Newborn Thunderbolt, Raw Thunderbolt and Heart of Earth. The collection of sea gods includes Heart of the Sea and Heart of the Lake, as well as gods named Begetter, Modeller, Bearer and Maker. This willingness to allow seemingly contradictory things to be true, in this case to allow each creator god to be both individual and also a group of many, is typical of Mesoamerican thought and mythology.

BOTH ONE AND TWO: AZTEC CREATION STORIES

The Plumed Serpent god played an important role in creation mythology of the Aztecs. He was not the Aztecs' primal or original creator, but he was one of the active deities who carried out the work of creation. According to the peoples of the Valley of Mexico, the supreme creator was Ometeotl, a god of duality

Below: This Aztec wooden mask depicts either rain god Tláloc or Quetzalcóatl as Éhecatl, lord of the winds.

Right: A terracotta image from Veracruz (c.AD500) represents a gruesome rite in honour of Xipe Totec, 'Our Flayed Lord'.

who existed in both male and female forms as Ometecuhtli and Omecíhuatl, twin gods who were also known as Tonacatecuhtli ('Lord of our Sustaining') and Tonacacíhuatl ('Lady of our Sustaining'). They lived in the thirteenth and highest level of the Aztec heaven, called Omeyocán.

BIRTH OF THE GODS

In one account, Tonacatecuhtli used his divine breath to bring life to a universe that was bathed in darkness. From his breath Quetzalcóatl was born, the Plumed Serpent as associated with the wind, particularly in his guise as Éhecatl. In another version, Omecíhuatl gave birth to all the gods and goddesses. In still another myth, the primal couple Ometecuhtli and Omecíhuatl gave birth to four gods, who they charged with the job of creating other deities, the world and the human race. They were the four Tezcatlipocas, each associated with a direction and a colour and some later identified with other gods.

Red Tezcatlipoca, connected to the east, was later identified as Xipe Totec, the god of vegetation and new life. Black Tezcatlipoca, associated with the night sky and the north, was later known simply as Tezcatlipoca. White Tezcatlipoca, associated with the west, was later known as Quetzalcóatl, while Blue Tezcatlipoca, linked to the south, was later Huitzilopochtli, the Aztec tribal god.

For six hundred years the four Tezcatlipocas delayed, then at last two of the gods, White Tezcatlipoca (Quetzalcóatl) and Blue Tezcatlipoca (Huitzilopochtli), began the ordained

Right: Chalchiúhtlicue, river goddess and consort of the rain god Tláloc, was praised for her power over the waters of spring.

work of creation. First they created fire and raised a forerunner of our sun in the sky. After this, they created the first human couple, Oxomoco and Cipactonal. They made the earth from a primal crocodile, the same creature later identified as the Earth Monster Tlaltecuhtli. From the crocodile's body they also fashioned the rain god Tláloc and his female counterpart Chalchiúhtlicue and they must also have made the underworld region of Mictlán, for the myth says they gave life to Mictlantecuhtli and Mictecacíhuatl, the god and goddess of the underworld. At this time they fixed the sacred calendar of the 260-day count. They also created Xochiquetzal ('Flower Feather'), goddess of flowers and the earth and of dance and love.

THE FIRST HUMANS AS GODS

Oxomoco and Cipactonal gave birth to a son named Piltzintecuhtli. He was the first human to enjoy the pleasures and duties of marriage, for he took as his wife a beautiful American maiden created by

Below: Images of Quetzalcóatl as the wind god Éhecatl characteristically have a bird-like mask on the lower face.

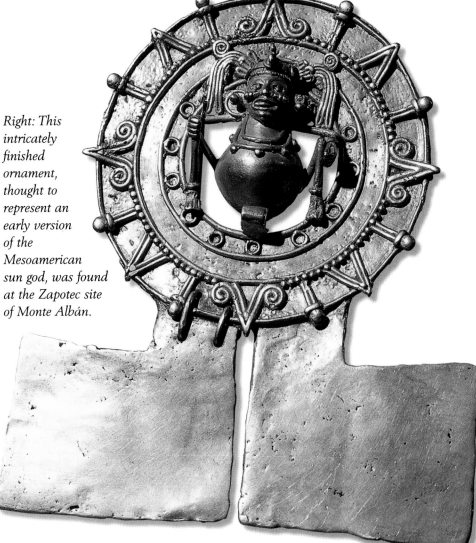

Right: This intricately finished ornament, thought to represent an early version of the Mesoamerican sun god, was found at the Zapotec site of Monte Albán.

the great gods from the hair of Xochiquetzal. The first human husband is sometimes identified as a god, and his consort is seen by some as a human incarnation of Xochiquetzal. After this creation, the gods began the four ages or 'suns' of the Earth's history.

Oxomoco and Cipactonal, the first humans, are similarly often viewed as gods. They played an important role in the myth that details the discovery and spread of the Mesoamericans' staple maize plant. According to this myth, the red ants had hidden maize deep inside Mount Tonacatépetl but Quetzalcóatl, bringer of so many good things to the human race, intuited that the ants' mountain store contained something of great value and transformed himself into a black ant to investigate. On the mountainside he tried out the limitations of his new body, clambering over rocks and into crevices, then followed the line of red ants along narrow paths within the mountain to

their hidden store. He found great piles of cereal there and carried some back to his brother gods. They tasted it and found it good, so they ground it up to make meal and placed some in the mouths of human babies. The babies thrived on this new food and the gods decreed that the maize should be shared with humans across the lands of Mesoamerica. But how would they free it from its hiding place? First Quetzalcóatl tied a great rope around the mountain and attempted to split the hard rock. But even the Plumed Serpent was not strong enough to bring down the mountain. The gods then turned to Oxomoco and Cipactonal for advice. The divine human couple consulted with one another and at last declared that the task should be entrusted to Nanahuatzin, the unappealing god who had become the Fifth Sun. He split the mountain and the rain god spirits or *tláloques* spread the maize far and wide.

THE ANGER OF THE GODS

The *Popol Vuh* of the Quiché Maya begins the tale of creation by describing the establishment of the fertile lands of the Earth, the gathering of the lakes and rivers that feed the soil and the springing to life of forests and life-giving plants. The account continues with the decision by the creator gods Huracán and Gucumatz to fill the Earth with animals and the first people.

They made animals to inhabit the mountains and forests, including deer and jaguars, snakes, pumas and birds. They appointed the creatures to their rightful places in the world, telling the deer to live in canyons along the banks of rivers and to roam freely in the fields and forests, while telling the birds to nest in the branches of trees and the safety of thick bushes. Then the creators called on the animals to speak to them and honour the gods who had given life to the forests and mountains. There were many names to choose from: Heart of Sky, Raw Thunderbolt, Hurricane, Plumed Serpent, Begetter, Maker, Modeller. But the animals could not speak a single name; all they could utter were wild cries, screeching and squawking. The gods were

Below: The toad was among the creatures created before the first people. This Classic Period Maya offering vessel dates from AD250–600.

not pleased, for what they wanted was a creature who was capable of keeping count of days and offering praise and sacrifices. They told the animals and birds that they would become food for each other and for the people whom the gods hoped to create.

MAN OF MUD?

Next the creators tried to make a human being from mud. However, try as they might, they could not make the body hold together: it kept sliding apart and dissolving into a watery mess. Its face was not pleasing, because it had a lopsided look and although the creature could speak, its words made no sense. The gods agreed to let the body dissolve. The man of mud was a false start and they decided to let it be a thought that led nowhere. However, they were determined to keep trying to create a human being. They decided next to consult an ancient pair of deities, divine equivalents of the

Above: This image of the Plumed Serpent god dates from 1300–1500. He was held in awe for his power to unleash floods.

'daykeepers' or shaman-diviners of the Quiché Maya. The couple were called Xpiyacoc and Xmucané. Huracán and Gucumatz addressed the couple as grandfather-grandmother, matchmaker-midwife, makers of jewellery and incense, carpenters and craftsmen.

MAN OF WOOD?

Huracán and Gucumatz asked the diviners whether human beings could be made from wood. The grandfather and grandmother performed a divination using kernels of corn and coral seeds and declared that wood was a suitable material for making people. They also warned Huracán against trying to trick Gucumatz. This aside perhaps reflects the gods' associations with forms of the Aztec deities Tezcatlipoca, linked to Huracán and always connected with deception and trickery, and Quetzalcóatl, linked to Gucumatz and in many myths the victim of Tezcatlipoca's plotting. Dennis Tedlock, the translator of the *Popol Vuh* and an initiated diviner, points out that Maya priests expect some trickery from the gods and will sometimes warn them in this way not to give a false answer during a divination.

Huracán and Gucumatz listened to the grandparents' reply and decided at once to fill the Earth with wooden people. 'Let it be so', they said, and their words were enough to make it happen; wooden people spread across the lands of America, the men made from the wood of the coral tree and the women made from the core of bulrushes. The people formed families and multiplied, but although they could speak, their hearts and minds were empty. They did not remember their creators or

Below: This late Classic Maya Period painted ceramic bowl decorated with a resting deer was found in El Petén, Guatemala.

count the days and honour the gods at the appropriate times. Moreover, although the people could walk and behave much like human beings, their skin was dry and flaky because they had no sweat, and their bodies warped in the heat because they had no blood to keep them moist.

AN UNMAKING

The gods determined to do away with this race of wooden people. Huracán sent powerful rainstorms that produced a vast flood and many people were drowned. To deal with the survivors, Huracán sent terrifying monsters, including Gouger of Faces, who carved out eyeballs, and Sudden Bloodletter, who pulled off their heads. The natural order the gods had established unravelled. Animals left their appointed places in the forests and on the mountains and invaded the houses

Above: Images of the Maya creator god Itzamná were often shown with crossed eyes.

of the people. The grinding stones, tortilla griddles and cooking pots rose up in violence and smashed the faces of the terrified people. The dogs they had kept attacked them. Even the hearthstones in the family fireplaces leapt out and set about the people's heads.

MONKEYS

The few survivors of the failed creation of the wooden people had battered heads and faces, but still looked a little like human beings. They were allowed to live on in the world in the form of monkeys. For this reason, the monkeys and apes of the forest resemble people. They are a reminder of a less than perfect creation. If humans forget their duty to mark the days, offer praise to the gods and seek the divine patterns in their lives, then they have become little better than the wooden people whose hearts and minds were empty.

Huracán and Gucumatz had now made three failed attempts to create a being capable of marking sacred days with a calendar and offering praise to the creators. They were still determined to keep trying, and their next attempt was destined to succeed.

THE HERO TWINS AND SEVEN MACAW

The *Popol Vuh* account digresses from the creation attempts of Huracán and Gucumatz in order to describe the valiant work of the divine Hero Twins in making earth and sky safe places. These events took place during the era of the wooden people.

A BID FOR POWER

In those days there was no day or night as we know it now, but only a long, unchanging twilight. Then a vain and boastful god called Seven Macaw tried to set himself up as supreme deity. He was a macaw and lived in a tree nest high above the earth of the wooden people. He had eyes of metal and teeth encrusted with turquoise and jewels, a great shiny nose and a nest of metal. Preening high

Below: An earthenware vase from Teotihuacán shows a quetzal bird in a cacao tree.

Below: Mesoamericans revered the tobacco plant and shredded its leaves to smoke in pipes such as this ceramic parrot.

in his tree, he declared that the light reflecting off his teeth was the blue of the sky while his nose could shine as brightly as the moon. He was also the sun, he said. When he came out in front of his shiny nest he gave light to the people below and his face shone far into the distance. The diviner-narrators of the *Popol Vuh* comment that, in truth Seven Macaw was none of these things, for as yet there was no sun or moon and the whole of creation existed in a half-light.

HERO TWINS

The young twin gods known as the Hero Twins, Hunahpú and Xbalanqué, discussed the behaviour of Seven Macaw and agreed that it was unacceptable for this vainglorious bird to puff himself up and claim to be greater than Gucumatz and Huracán, the wise modellers and makers who had created the world by the power of their spoken word. The twins were the children of the god Hun Hunahpú and Blood Moon, a maiden of the under-world. Both the twins were skilled hunters and went far and wide shooting birds and animals with their blowpipes. They decided to use their hunting skills to puncture Seven Macaw's pride. One morning the twins lay in wait for Seven Macaw beneath a tree where the bird came each day to feed. Hunahpú waited until the macaw was busy eating, then used his blowpipe to deliver an accurate shot that broke Seven Macaw's jaw. The bird fell from the tree and Hunahpú ran across the ground to seize it but, just as he arrived, Seven Macaw caught hold of his arm and wrenched it from its socket. Hunahpú was left in agony, with blood pouring from his wound, while Seven Macaw went slowly home, ruminating over the damage to his jaw. His wife Chimalmat greeted him, expressing surprise at his appearance, and he described the sudden attack that had broken his jaw and given him an almighty toothache. However, he had a trophy from the conflict, he said, and held up Hunahpú's arm. He hung the arm above his fire and declared that the trickster twins could come and get it if they wanted it.

PUNCTURED PRIDE

Hunahpú and Xbalanqué now devised a plan for outwitting Seven Macaw. They approached Great White Peccary and Great White Tapir, a wise grandfather and grandmother, for help. The twins proposed that the old couple should approach the boastful macaw pretending to be travelling medics and offer to ease his pain. Hunahpú and Xbalanqué would travel with them in the guise of their grandchildren. The bird would probably beg for help and then, once his guard was down, the elderly couple and the twins could strip him of his finery and retrieve

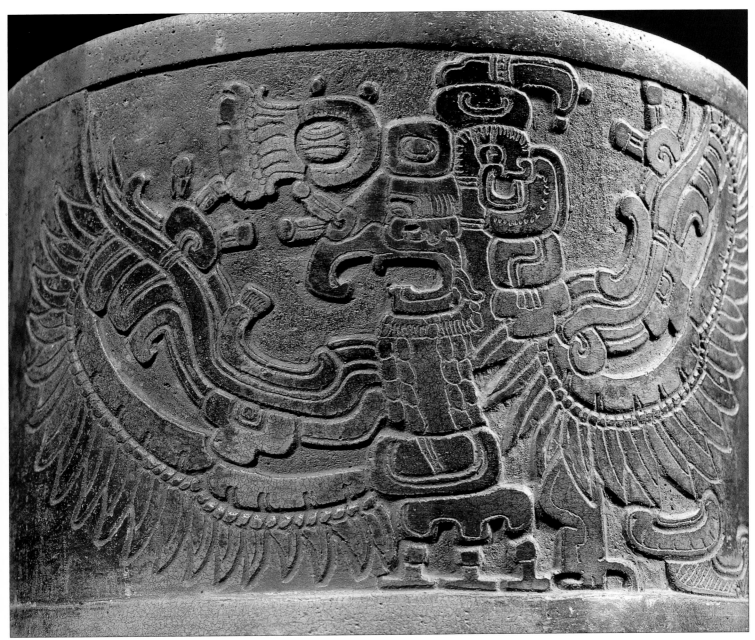

Above: This detail of a clay vase dating from c.AD200–400 shows Seven Macaw wearing a necklace that denotes his power.

Hunahpú's arm. Great White Peccary and Great White Tapir agreed to the deception and they went, with the twins in tow, to Seven Macaw's splendid home.

The plan worked exactly as the twins had hoped. The grandparents persuaded Seven Macaw his toothache was caused by worms gnawing in his mouth and that it would ease if he let them extract his jewel-entrusted teeth and replace them with new ones of the finest ground bone. But the 'teeth' they put in his mouth were just corn kernels. Next, while he was still under their control, they removed the precious metal from around his eyes.

The battle was now won. Seven Macaw grew weaker and weaker as his finery was stripped from him and at last he died. His wife Chimalmat, who was seemingly weakened by his decline, expired at his side. It was a simple task for Great White Peccary and Great White Tapir and the Hero Twins to retrieve Hunahpú's arm from Seven Macaw's fireplace. The aged couple then proved that they did have genuine medical skill by putting Hunahpú's arm back in place so that it was perfectly healed.

Seven Macaw's likeness can still be seen on Earth in the scarlet macaw, which has a strangely shaped beak with a larger upper part and smaller lower part, suggesting the image of the dislocated jaw. It also has featherless patches around the eyes, which resemble the bare region surrounding the god's eyes after his face had been stripped of its shining metals.

Left: A late Classic Period Maya censer, sanctified by the face of the sun god, from the Temple of the Cross, Palenque.

25

THE TRIUMPH OF THE HERO TWINS

Seven Macaw had two sons, boys who were as self-deceiving and boastful as their father. One, Zipacná, named himself 'Maker of Mountains' and claimed to have raised the great peaks of the early world that had in fact been created by Huracán and Gucumatz. The second son, Earthquake, said he could unseat the foundations of the world and bring everything crashing down in an avalanche of earth. The Hero Twins, having dealt with Seven Macaw, decided to rid the world of his arrogant offspring too.

ZIPACNÁ'S DOWNFALL

The Hero Twins made their move against Zipacná at a time when the Maker of Mountains had not eaten for several days. In normal times, Zipacná's favourite diet was crabs and fish and he spent his hours trawling the waters and lifting huge rocks – even mountains – to see if any crabs were underneath. The Twins built a mechanical crab from flowers and a rock and placed it in a crevice beneath a great

Below: A Maya polychrome vase depicts the Hero Twin Hunahpú with stern expression, magnificent headdress and regal bearing.

GODS OF DRUNKENNESS

Before the Hero Twins turned their attention to Zipacná, the 'Maker of Mountains' had a bruising encounter with the Four Hundred Boys, the gods of a strong alcoholic drink called *quii* by the Quiché Maya.

The Four Hundred Boys met Zipacná on the seashore as they were dragging along a huge log which they had cut to use as a doorpost for their house. Zipacná offered to help and lifted the great trunk on his own, carrying it all the way to the house. The Four Hundred Boys asked him to stay with them to help them the next day, but secretly they plotted to kill him, for they were frightened by his enormous strength and guessed that they could not trust him.

The Four Hundred Boys dug a deep hole and enticed Zipacná into it. When he was at the bottom, they dropped a log on top of him. They thought they had killed him and rejoiced, planning a great celebration with the *quii* drink. They would wait, they said, for two

days. When ants swarmed in the hole and carried parts of Zipacná's body to the surface they would know for certain that he was dead and they would have their party.

However, Zipacná had scrambled out of the way of the log and lay at the bottom of the hole listening to their every word. Two days later, when the ants came to investigate, Zipacná handed them tufts of his hair and pieces of his nails and told them to carry them to the surface. The Four Hundred Boys saw the ants and whooped for joy. They went into their new house and toasted their own bravery, jeering at Zipacná. Soon they all became very drunk and unruly. Zipacná crept from the hole and knocked the house down around the drunkards. Every one of the Four Hundred Boys was killed and Zipacná had his revenge.

The Four Hundred Boys, who were revered as the gods of drunkenness, rose into the sky and became the constellation of the Pleiades.

mountain, then casually approached Zipacná on the beach. When he complained of his hunger, they mentioned that they had seen the biggest of crabs in the crevice nearby. He followed them and went eagerly into the crevice in search of his next meal. However, try as he might he could not reach the crab until he turned over on to his back. At this point, with the mechanical crab on his chest, he suddenly expired and his body turned to stone. For all his bravado and undoubted strength, the genius of the Hero Twins had brought him low.

EARTHQUAKE'S UNDOING

Next, the sky god Huracán talked to the Hero Twins, asking them to deal with Zipacná's brother Earthquake. When

CHAPTER TWO

EARTH AND SKY

Mesoamericans believed that the age we live in was not the first in the history of the world. Just as the Quiché Maya told that there had been other, failed creations before the making of the first people by the sky god Huracán and the sea god Gucumatz, so the Aztecs held that there had been previous world ages before our own. The current age, in the Aztec view, was the fifth.

Each of these five eras had its own sun, was associated with one of the elements and was presided over by a different god. The celebrated Aztec Sun Stone, discovered in the late 18th century beneath Mexico City's central plaza, depicts each of the five 'suns'. Its main face, 3.6m (almost 12ft) in diameter, has a head in the centre, representing either the ancient sun god Tonatiuh or the Earth Monster Tlaltecuhtli. Around this face in the central circle are four images in square frames. The one to the upper right represents the first sun, that of the jaguar, while the one to the upper left shows the second sun, that of the wind. The one to the lower left is for the third sun, of rain, and the one to the lower right refers to the fourth sun, of water. The central face celebrates the current sun or world age in which the Aztecs had risen to such glory. Scholars also link the four suns to the four directions of Aztec cosmology. According to this theory, the Fifth Sun represents the centre.

Left: The Sun Stone was probably carved during the rule of Axayácatl (1469–81), with the aim of validating Aztec rule. The 'people of the sun' were divinely sanctioned to govern.

LIFE UNDER THE FOUR SUNS

In the primordial era, Black Tezcatlipoca decided to set himself up as the sun. This god was one of the 'four Tezcatlipocas' associated with the primal creation, each of whom was linked to a god in the Aztec pantheon. He was linked to the god of night and destiny later worshipped as Tezcatlipoca. His age, or sun, began after the time of the initial creation, when White Tezcatlipoca (Quetzalcóatl) and Blue Tezcatlipoca (Huitzilopochtli) made fire, the first human couple and several of the other gods.

THE JAGUAR SUN

Black Tezcatlipoca rose into the sky. His era was associated with the element of earth. There were no humans; instead the lands of Mesoamerica were filled by a race of giants. These towering creatures were so strong they could rip trees from the rocky mountain ground and hurl them through the air down on to the dusty plain below. But they were not bloodthirsty and lived on a vegetarian diet of acorns. Black Tezcatlipoca's era lasted 676 years. It ended in a cataclysm when Quetzalcóatl grew displeased at seeing Tezcatlipoca in the height of the sacred sky. He used his staff to knock his rival down into the seas that lay at the farthest extremes of the flat earth.

In his anger, Black Tezcatlipoca rose from the salt waters in the form of a powerful jaguar. The sun was down and darkness covered the land. Tezcatlipoca, god of night, raced on to the plains and mountains of Mesoamerica and suddenly jaguars were running everywhere. A plague of the fierce night predators howled for blood. The jaguars hunted down the giants and killed every one. According to the Aztecs' complex calendar, this carnage occurred on the day 4-Jaguar in the year 1-Reed.

Because jaguars brought the age or sun to an end, it is usually named the 'Jaguar Sun' (*Nahui Ocelotl*); it is also sometimes called the '4-Jaguar Sun' after the day on

which it ended. All the four suns would end in a cataclysm of violence and death and each one was named after the terrible event that brought it to an end. Tezcatlipoca himself leapt into the sky, still in his jaguar form, and there made the constellation of the Great Bear.

THE WIND SUN

Quetzalcóatl created the second sun, which provided light for the next age of the world.

This era was associated with the air and Quetzalcóatl took his form as the wind god Éhecatl to perform the creation. The inhabitants of Mesoamerica in this age were more like modern humans than their primitive predecessors. They also followed a vegetarian diet, eating the seeds of the mesquite tree. The second age lasted 364 years. Tezcatlipoca

Above: A detail from an Aztec stone column depicts the head of Tláloc, rain god and creator of the third sun.

revenged himself on his great cosmic rival by bringing this age to an end. He used his dark power to overwhelm the wind god by launching a great hurricane that swept the sun from the sky and the people from the earth. Darkness fell once more on the lands of Mesoamerica and after the hurricane everything was suddenly still. The survivors clambered up into the branches of the few trees that were still standing after the storm. They were no longer people but had become monkeys and they chattered and called in the echoing dark. The era ended on the day 4-Wind in the year 1-Flint. The sun or world age is known as the 'Wind Sun' (*Nahui Éhecatl*) or 'Sun 4-Wind'. The

Aztec myth parallels the account of the Quiché Maya in the *Popol Vuh*, in which the survivors of a failed creation, the wooden people, were the ancestors of the monkeys of the forest.

THE RAIN SUN

After the hurricane, the fertility and rain god Tláloc took charge of creation. His era was associated with the element of fire. In some accounts, the people of this age made one of the great breakthroughs in human history by discovering the skills of agriculture and began to cultivate a form of maize. In other versions, however, the people lived entirely on a wild water-based plant like the water lily. Then they were transformed from human form into turkeys, dogs and butterflies.

Tláloc's era lasted 312 years before Quetzalcóatl again turned destroyer. This time, he sent a rain of fire that poured destruction on the earth for a whole day. The inferno of flame swept the sun from the sky. The inhabitants were burned up, but some must have hidden from the fire, for their descendants are the dogs, butterflies and turkeys of today. The destruction came on the day 4-Rain in the year 1-Flint. This sun or age is called 'Rain Sun' (*Nahui Quiahuitl*) or 'Sun

Left: Images of the rain god Tláloc are usually identifiable from their 'goggle' eyes and fang-like teeth.

Right: A wooden inlaid mask honours Chalchiúhtlicue, creator of the fourth world age.

4-Rain', but is also sometimes called the 'Fire Sun' because this era of creation ended in a firestorm. The coming of fire from the sky was an appropriate ending for Tláloc's era, for this god, in addition to being the deity of rain, was associated with lightning – a form of celestial fire.

THE WATER SUN

Tláloc's consort Chalchiúhtlicue, goddess of lakes, oceans, streams and rivers, created a new sun. The people of the age of water lived on the seeds of a wild plant. Chalchiúhtlicue's era lasted 676 years; as long as the previous two eras combined, and was the first of the world ages in which the presiding deity herself brought creation to an end.

The Aztecs believed that the waters of the oceans enclosed the lands on all four sides and also rose up into the sky above. In one account, Chalchiúhtlicue made these sky waters break so that they crashed down and obliterated life on earth. In another version, she made the underground waters rise up, gushing from natural wells and bursting from solid rock. Either way, a great flood covered the land. The people adapted, turning into fish, whales and other inhabitants of the deep.

The flood lasted for an entire 'bundle' of 52 years. Even the mountains were swept away, as water covered the entire creation. The flood came on the day 4-Water in the year 1-House. The era was therefore called 'Water Sun' (*Nahui Atl*) or 'Sun 4-Water'.

There is some disagreement in different sources over the order in which the suns or ages occurred. The sequence given here of Jaguar, Wind, Rain and Water is that depicted in the carvings on the Aztec Sun Stone, a 3.6m- (almost 12ft-) wide carved stone found in Mexico City in the 18th century. Some other sources report that the Water Sun came first and that the other three followed in the sequence Jaguar, Rain, Wind. The end of the fourth sun was the occasion for the creation of the current world age, the fifth sun, the time in which the Aztecs, their revered Toltec ancestors and modern Mexicans all live.

The Quiché Maya account of creation also included the notion that previous creations had their own suns that lapsed when the creation failed. For example, the vain bird Seven Macaw who was outwitted and defeated by the Hero Twins Hunahpú and Xbalanqué was the Sun in the era of the wooden people.

DAWN OF THE FIFTH SUN

Following the end of the fourth sun or age in a great earthquake, Tezcatlipoca and Quetzalcóatl had to fashion the Earth anew. They encountered the Earth Monster Tlaltecuhtli swimming in the waters of the great flood and by tearing apart her body they made a new sky and a new earth.

A period of 26 years passed between the creation of a new world for the fifth sun and the creation of the sun and moon that ushered in the age in which we live.

Below: The ancient fire god Xiuhtecuhtli was generally depicted without eyes, seated with arms crossed on his knees.

Like the four previous ages, the fifth era was named after the cataclysm that would bring it to an end. The Aztecs believed that the current age would end in earthquakes; they also said that the current sun began moving on the day 4-Ollin (4-Earthquake or 4-Movement), and that the world would end on the day 4-Earthquake. On that fateful day the god Tezcatlipoca would once more fulfil his dark destiny as a destroyer, sending earthquakes that would bring the mountains low and cause a famine in which all creatures would die. The Aztecs named the age in which we live after this day of destruction, 4-Ollin.

CREATION OF THE SUN AND THE MOON

The Aztec myth of the creation of the sun and moon tells how the gods gathered in darkness at Teotihuacán. There was no light on the earth, for the fourth sun had been destroyed in the watery cataclysm that brought an end to Chalchiúhtlicue's era. The gods were voices in the blank darkness. They agreed that what was most necessary for the creation was a new sun and a moon to provide light when the sun did not.

The god Tecuciztécatl ('He of the Sea Stone') stepped forward and volunteered to be the sun. But a second deity also volunteered. This was the small and humble god Nanahuatzin, whose

Above: Some scholars identify this Aztec stone carving as an image of a priest in the service of the fire god Xiuhtecuhtli.

face was disfigured by pimples and sores. These two began to prepare themselves for the honour of lighting the world with rites of penitence and self-discipline like those of a new Aztec *tlatoani* or ruler before he took power. Nanahuatzin and Tecuciztécatl prepared for four days and nights. When they were finished, they saw that the other gods had lit a vast pyre on the hard ground at Teotihuacán. The orange flames threw unsettling shadows all around that holy place.

Nanahuatzin and Tecuciztécatl made offerings: the self-regarding Tecuciztécatl, dressed in splendid robes, offered fine goods such as quetzal feathers, stone flints and coral incense, while the humble and self-effacing Nanahuatzin laid out simple reeds, cactus thorns he had used to make an offering of his own blood and, instead of incense, the scabs from his pimples. They approached the sacred fire. Tecuciztécatl went first, but was driven back by the heat. He tried again, and a second time did not have the courage or resolve to carry through his intention of entering the flames. In all, he approached the fire and turned back four times. Then Nanahuatzin stepped forward. He shut his eyes and steadied his nerves with deep breaths, then went fearlessly into the flames. The other gods watched in awe as his body caught, crackled and burned fast. At last, inspired by his rival, Tecuciztécatl rushed into the flames. An eagle and a jaguar followed the two gods into the flames, so gaining their distinctive markings and their reputation for fearlessness and power.

A NEW AGE

The sacrifice was complete. The other gods waited for the first day of the new age to begin. In one account, the proud

Below: The Cerro Gordo peak behind gives Teotihuacán's Pyramid of the Moon the look of a natural formation.

but fearful Tecuciztécatl rose first into the sky in the form of the moon, shining very brilliantly. He was followed by Nanahuatzin, the new sun. In another version, the new sun and moon rose together. In both accounts the light of the moon was too bright and cancelled out that of the sun. One of the gods on the ground threw a rabbit up at the moon's face, giving the moon its distinctive markings, in which Mesoamericans saw the shape of a rabbit.

The sun and moon hung in the sky, motionless and lifeless. This was not as it should be. How could time progress and the seasons be measured if there were no movements in the heavens? Nanahuatzin made an announcement

Left: All life came from the gods' initial sacrifice. This sacrificial knife, made of wood and flint, dates from c.1500.

from his position at his zenith in the sky. He would consent to follow the required daily motions of the sun, but only if the other gods offered their hearts and lifeblood in sacrifice, as he had made an offering of his earthly body. At first the gods on the ground were outraged and one, the morning star, attacked Nanahuatzin, but then they agreed to make the first of the many blood sacrifices that maintained the flow of life-energy in the Mesoamerican cosmos. They cut their own bodies and offered their hearts to the sun. The sun began to move and the moon sank behind the Earth's horizon.

THE CELESTIAL WEAVING GIRL

Other Mesoamerican myths explain how the sky and earth were separated and the moon and sun were brought into being. A Mixtec tale recounted that Lord Nine Wind, a god associated with the Aztec deity Quetzalcóatl, separated the waters and the Earth, using the waters to make a sky that would arch over and contain the land.

PARALLELS

Quiché Maya mythology in the *Popol Vuh* tells that water and sky were always already separate: the sky god and the sea god cooperated to make the earth after a

Below: Mesoamerican myths told that the sun, here honoured on a Maya pyramid, first rose above a well-established Earth.

Right: This terracotta mask may represent the ancient Maya counterpart to the Aztec fire god.

fruitful discussion of what would be right. In the Quiché tradition, the sun and moon were created later, when the Hero Twins Hunahpú and Xbalanqué rose up into the heavens after their successful mission to the underworld. The Quiché Maya and Aztec creation myths therefore both put some time between the creation of the Earth in its current age and the rising of the sun and moon to give light.

THE EARTH MONSTER'S BODY

In the Aztec myth, Quetzalcóatl and Tezcatlipoca made the Earth from the Earth Monster's body and Quetzalcóatl made the first people some time before the sun and moon were made by the gods' sacrifice at Teotihuacán. In one version of the Aztec myth there were 26 years between the creation of the Earth and the first appearance of the sun.

This myth explains that the waters of the heavens fell, unleashing the great flood that swept away the fourth sun in the year 1-Toctli (1-Rabbit), which was associated with the south. Quetzalcóatl and Tezcatlipoca made the Earth and then Tezcatlipoca assumed a new identity as Mixcóatl, an ancient hunt god sometimes said to be god of the north. This happened in the year (2-Ácatl) 2-Reed. In the diviners' calendar, the day named 2-Reed was sacred to Tezcatlipoca. The next period began on the year 1-Ácatl (1-Reed). It was sacred to Quetzalcóatl, one of whose attributes was as god of the east. The gods made the sun 13 years

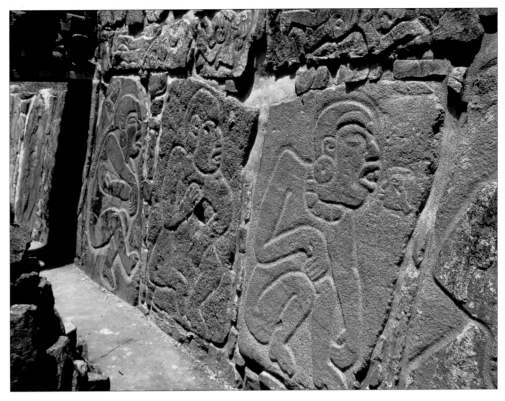

afterwards, in 13-Ácatl (13-Reed). This sequence suggests how Mesoamerican myths are intimately connected to the day-names, year-names and other timings of the sacred calendar, as well as to the movements of the stars and planets.

A LOVE STORY

A different Maya tradition explained the relationship between the sun and moon and their ascension to the sky in terms of an earthly love story and explains thereby the origins of human sexual relations. At one time, according to this story, the sun and moon lived on Earth: Sun was a sturdy young hunter and Moon a fair maiden who earned her corn bread by working as a weaver. Sun fell for the pale, luminous beauty of Moon the moment he first saw her and he was drawn back to her grandfather's house again and again to try to catch a glimpse of her peaceful face. Every morning Sun arrived at the house, carrying a vast deer carcass on his shoulders in an attempt to impress the maiden with his strength and hunting prowess. But although Moon was pleased by the attention and began to have feelings for the hunter, her grandfather was against the relationship and did all he could to prevent it flowering into love.

Now Sun had magical powers as well as virile strength and he transformed himself into a hummingbird. In this shape he

could come and go as he pleased without the maiden's grandfather seeing, and he loved to haunt the garden behind the old man's house, where tobacco plants grew. The maiden, either displeased by the attentions of the hummingbird or guessing its true identity, had her grandfather shoot the swift-winged bird in flight. In the moment he was shot, the hummingbird reverted back into human form. The moon-maiden then nursed Sun back to health, keeping his identity secret from her grandfather. When Sun was well again, she fled with him.

PREVENTING AN ELOPEMENT

Now other gods joined in to try and prevent the elopement. Spying them in a canoe on the river far below, the rain god hurled a thunderbolt at the pair. Sun changed himself into a turtle and Moon transformed herself into a crab, but for Moon it was too late. She was broken into many pieces and died.

Grieving, Sun collected the remains of his love and, with the help of a band of dragonflies, stored them in thirteen hollow logs. He waited for thirteen days,

Left: Mixtecs, proud of their creative skills, believed that from the beginning their gods were blessed with genius in fine arts, metalworking and other crafts.

Above: The Zapotecs, makers of the enigmatic figures thought to be slain war captives at Monte Albán, taught that there were separate creators of animals (made by Cozaana) and men (made by Huichaana).

then opened the logs. The first twelve logs were filled with poisonous snakes and angry insects, which fled into the world and have been an unpleasant and sometimes deadly presence ever since. But in the thirteenth log, by a thoroughly breathtaking miracle, he found the Moon maiden, restored to life. Now a deer was passing and stamped on the moon through the log, creating the very first female sexual organ. Sun and Moon then had sexual relations. This was the first time male and female had combined in this perfect complementarity.

Once again the lovers were united. They lived for many more years on Earth but Sun discovered that he could not trust his love, who had a carnal nature. She took many lovers when his attention was elsewhere and in his anger and desperate, continuing love he took her with him into exile in the sky. In one tradition, his anger and fear of her sexual happiness made him attack her, blinding her in one eye. For this reason the light given by the moon is weaker by far than that given by the sun.

MYTHS OF THE NIGHT SKY

The gods and heroes of Mesoamerican mythology were visible in the night sky. The movements of the stars and planets gave solid form to the repeating cycles of the myths. The stories of many deities ended with their ascension to the night sky to take the form of this or that group of stars, and the rising, falling and other movements of the constellations were a regular reminder of the truth of the myths and of the divine transactions that sustained life.

ASTRONOMY AND THE GODS

The movements of the stars were also connected to farmers' cycles of planting and reaping, for astronomical phenomena were used to time the agricultural cycle. For example, in the Quiché Maya *Popol Vuh* cycle, the early humans known as the Four Hundred Boys were killed by Zipacná, son of the boastful solar deity Seven Macaw. At their death they rose into the sky to become the Pleiades

Above: One face of the Aztec altar of the nocturnal animals shows an owl. The other sides depict a bat, a scorpion and a spider.

constellation. In Quiché lore, the Pleiades were associated with a handful of seeds. Dennis Tedlock, translator of the *Popol Vuh*, points out that the period in March when high-altitude farmers plant maize is marked by the setting of the Pleiades in the evening. When the lower altitude maize is planted in May, the Pleiades are completely invisible. The disappearance of the Four Hundred Boys of the Pleiades marks the time when the maize seeds 'disappear' into the earth and later the constellation is visible again as the seeds 'dawn' in the form of plants.

Seven Macaw became the seven stars that make up the Plough or Big Dipper. In the latitude of the Quiché Maya, the seasonal disappearance of this constellation appears to usher in the rainy storms of the hurricane season. In mid-July, at the start of the hurricane season, the Plough can be seen descending at twilight and afterwards disappears for much of the night. In mid-October the reappearance of all seven stars of the constellation before dawn marks the end of the hurricanes and the start of the dry season. In the myth, the god's fall from the tree when he is shot by Hunahpú occurs just before the great flood that is sent against the wooden people. In the same way, the descent of Seven Macaw's constellation brings the waters of the rainy hurricane season.

CYCLICAL MOVEMENTS

The *Popol Vuh* cycle is entirely built on the cyclical movements of the stars and planets – especially the Venus cycle – and on the sacred calendar that is derived from them. Before the Hero Twins are born, their father and uncle One and Seven Hunahpú are summoned to the underworld because their playing of the Mesoamerican ball game makes such a racket that it annoys the underworld lords. This corresponds to a day named Hunahpú in the calendar and to the rising of Venus as the morning star in the eastern sky. One and Seven Hunahpú then descend to the underworld, where they play ball against the underworld

Below: This vast Aztec stone head is of the moon goddess Coyolxauhqui, with her characteristic lunar nose pendant.

Above: Quetzalcóatl descends to Earth in his most familiar guise, as the Plumed Serpent.

Right: This small clay idol may be Xólotl, Quetzalcóatl's form as Venus the evening star.

lords. This corresponds to the time in the Venus cycle when the planet is not visible. When One Hunahpú is killed, this equates to the reappearance of Venus as the evening star. When an underworld maiden, Blood Woman, becomes pregnant with One Hunahpú's sons (the Hero Twins) and climbs to the Earth's surface, she convinces One Hunahpú's mother, Xmucané, that she has come from the underworld pregnant with the sons of One Hunahpú. This corresponds to the new rising of Venus as the morning star. In addition, One Monkey and One Artisan, the half-brothers of the Hero Twins, correspond to the planet Mars. Their names are both associated with the day in the diviners' calendar when Mars becomes visible.

Aztec myths were similarly tied into astronomical movements. Tezcatlipoca brought the first sun or world age to an end by unleashing the rage of the night predator, the jaguar. He then rose in the sky in the form of a great celestial jaguar and became the Great Bear constellation. When the Great Bear dips into the sea, Aztec stargazers understood it to mark the moment in the cosmic myth of the world's creation when Tezcatlipoca lost a foot in his struggle with the Earth Monster, Tlaltecuhtli.

Quetzalcóatl's myth closely parallels the Venus cycle. In one tradition, after being outwitted by the followers of Tezcatlipoca in Tollán and subsequently disgraced, he sacrificed himself on a pyre and his soul rose as Venus. In this guise he was known as Ce Ácatl and Tlahuizcalpantecuhtli (Dawn), and understood to be an enemy of the sun. When Quetzalcóatl made a voyage to the underworld to collect the bones of the fish-men of the fourth world age, he was Venus during its invisible phase and when he returned in triumph with the bones to make a new race of men he was Venus rising again as the morning star.

MANY FACES OF THE SUN GOD

The Aztecs thought of themselves as the people of the sun. At Teotihuacán, the gods had performed the first blood sacrifice to set the sun and moon in motion in the sky, but the ritual did not prove sufficient to feed the blood-hungry sun. Fortunately, the Aztec people and their neighbours were able to take on the task of feeding the sun and maintaining its daily movements through war and blood sacrifice.

AZTEC DAWN

Each dawn was a time of trepidation. The moment of transition between dark and light might be the world's last, for if the sun refused to move across the sky then there would be no day, no time and no seasons to mark with the calendar. To ensure that the sun was sufficiently nourished, Aztec priests had to follow the religious calendar with the utmost devotion and make all the appropriate sacrifices at the right time.

The Aztecs believed that the sun took different forms at different times of day and night. An ancient god named Tonatiuh was the sun by day. Each dawn, as he rose from the eastern horizon, he was born anew of the earth goddess Coatlícue. In one tradition he was hauled up to the zenith of the sky by the souls of brave warriors who had died in battle. For this honour the souls took the form of hummingbirds. The Aztecs saw Tonatiuh as a strong, vibrant young man with an ochre and yellow-painted face and a red-painted body. He was guided across the sky by a great fire-serpent called the *xiuhcóatl*.

Some accounts reveal that at its zenith, when the sun is most powerful, it changed from Tonatiuh to the Aztec tribal god Huitzilopochtli. At noon, beneath the brilliance of Huitzilopochtli, darkness

Left: This clay pipe with its eagle's head celebrates the daily triumph of the sun god. The Aztecs thought tobacco – which they called yetl – *was sacred. Pipes in the image of the sun god were probably used by his priests.*

was entirely vanquished. With the sun directly overhead there were not even any shadows to remind men of the encroaching coldness and the many demons of night.

After noon, as the sun descended towards his nightly disappearance at dusk, he was pulled down the length of sky by the *cilhuateteo*, the souls of women who had died in childbirth, slain by unborn warriors in the womb. At dusk, as he sank beyond the horizon, he was understood to be devoured by the Earth Monster Tlaltecuhtli.

A JAGUAR BY NIGHT

By night, the sun travelled through the dread realms of the underworld, Mictlán. During these hours, Tonatiuh took the shape of Tepeyolohtli, a jaguar named 'Heart of the Hard Mountain'. The roaring of this great beast, who was caged within the mountain, could be heard in the thundering of avalanches and the noisy eruption of volcanic lava.

The jaguar was a night predator, capable of striking suddenly and fatally in the blackness of the wild countryside and so the jaguar was naturally associated with the night and with the dark underworld. In some traditions, the sun defeated his enemies in the underworld each night with the *xiuhcóatl* or fire-serpent.

Left: An Aztec codex depicts preparations for a sacrifice in the sun god's honour at the pyramid-top temple halfway to the sky.

Right: The Maya sun god Kinich Ahau was the husband of the moon goddess Ix Chel. At night, as he travelled through the underworld, it was believed that he turned into a jaguar.

The Classic Period Maya also believed that the sun became a jaguar by night. By day they thought the life-giving star was a male god named Kinich Ahau ('Sun-faced Lord'), a fresh-faced young man at dawn who aged during the long day and who, by dusk, had an old man's face and beard. In carvings and pictures, he is depicted with a fierce face and a single front tooth. On his forehead is often carved the four-petalled glyph for *kin*, which means 'day' or 'sun'. A fine stucco mask of the god survives among the remains of the main pyramid at the Maya site of Kohunlich in the Mexican state of Quintana Roo.

After dusk, the Maya sun god was reborn in the first moments of night as a jaguar who travelled through the underworld, where he had to do battle – like the Hero Twins and the souls of the dead – with the lords of Xibalba. Some images of Kinich Ahau prefigure this night-time transformation by depicting the day-sun god with the characteristics or features of a jaguar. A number of representations of the jaguar god of the underworld show him with the *kin* glyph ('sun' or 'day') on his sleek stomach.

DARKNESS AND LIGHT

Night was also a time to be feared. The Aztecs believed that Tezcatlipoca was at large in the hours of darkness, sometimes taking the form of a headless demon called Night Axe, sometimes of a wandering demon who approached travellers at the crossroads. It was also the time and the realm of the demons called *tzitimime*, female spirits who sparkled with malevolence like stars in the blue darkness. They were responsible for unleashing many of the ills that afflicted humankind, such as the epidemics that swept through the Valley of Mexico after the Spanish Conquest. Their power was at its height when night encroached upon day in the form of a solar eclipse. At these times the Aztecs made sacrifices of fair-skinned victims to fortify Tonatiuh in his weakness.

The opposition between darkness and light was central to Mesoamerican mythology. Whereas Tezcatlipoca was associated with dark, his eternal rival and counterpart Quetzalcóatl was linked to dawn. Quetzalcóatl was associated with the east and, in his aspect as Tlahuizcalpantecuhtli, with Venus as the morning star that heralded the sunrise. His rising symbolized resurrection while the darkness of Tezcatlipoca stood for death. The ball game played throughout Mesoamerica may have been seen as a re-enactment of the struggles between Tezcatlipoca and Quetzalcóatl that were such an important part of the myth of the four suns before our own; of struggles in the Aztecs' lives between darkness and light, between death and life. The balance between light and dark also corresponded to the opposition between dryness and dampness, height and smallness and, in some instances, between masculinity and femininity.

Below: An image from the Codex Borbonicus *shows the sun god (left) in the form he assumed by night.*

BRINGERS OF RAIN

One version of the Aztec myth of the creation of the sun and moon gave a vital role to Éhecatl, the wind god who was an aspect of Quetzalcóatl. After the gods Nanahuatzin and Tecuciztécatl had thrown themselves on to the sacrificial pyre and ascended into the sky as sun and moon, they hung motionless above the Earth. In this tradition, it was Éhecatl who initiated their movements. He blew on them with all the strength of his breath. At first, only the sun moved and the moon remained stationary, but when the sun set at last in the west the moon was drawn into his proper cycle, which complements that of the sun.

Below: At Chichén Itzá, the ruined tower of the Caracol – perhaps a temple to wind god Kukulcán as well as an astronomical observatory – contained a spiral corridor.

In contrast to other gods, who were generally associated with a particular point of the compass, Éhecatl was linked to all four directions because the wind blows from the north, south, east and west. Temples built to honour the god were partly circular in form. A circular temple to Éhecatl-Quetzalcóatl reputedly stood opposite the great temple of the Aztecs in Tenochtitlán. Éhecatl was associated with, and at times represented as, a spider monkey, a duck, a spider and a snail. Statues of him often wear a half-mask with the appearance of a duck's bill, open to allow the tongue to show.

Left: This stone carving of Éhecatl-Quetzalcóatl has obsidian eyes. The god blew through his beak to make the winds.

Scholars believe the Aztecs associated the spider monkey with the wind because of its great speed and agility when swinging through the trees. Another connection is that, at the end of the fourth age, humans were destroyed by a great wind and turned into monkeys. Quetzalcóatl in the guise of Éhecatl was patron of the second day in the Aztecs' day-count calendar.

Above: This dancing monkey honours the power of the wind god Éhecatl-Quetzalcóatl. The snake suggests the whirlwinds with which Éhecatl ushered in the rainy season.

THE BREATH OF LIFE

The wind unleashed by Éhecatl-Quetzalcóatl was the breath of life itself for, without the setting and rising of the sun, there would be no seasons, no cycles of planting and harvesting, no crops and no life in Mesoamerica. The god blew the damp winds that carried rain clouds to the grateful farmers at the start of the rainy season. He also unleashed whirlwinds that cleared the skies for the clouds. For this reason the Aztecs called him 'the *tláloques*' road-sweeper' – a reference to the little rain gods who were assistants to the main rain deity, Tláloc.

An illustration in the *Vienna Codex* shows Éhecatl connecting earth and sky and supporting the clouds above.

An Aztec sculpture also depicts Quetzalcóatl rising, serpentine, from the earth-mother to connect with the rain god Tláloc above. It was all part of the Aztecs' cosmological view that the rains were present in the sky above because the sea that lay at the far extremes of the earth curved up to join over it.

The connection provided between the earth and the sky by Éhecatl-Quetzalcóatl was necessary to provide a conduit or pathway by which the waters could return to the earth in the form of windblown rainclouds.

KUKULCÁN-QUETZALCÓATL

The wind god was worshipped as Kukulcán by the central and northern Maya, while the southern Maya knew him as Gucumatz. The wind god was associated with the rain god Chac as bringer of fertility.

Some scholars believe that the circular Caracol at Chichén Itzá, while certainly an astronomical observatory, may also have served as a temple to the god Kukulcán-Quetzalcóatl. Its circular shape means that the building was probably sacred to the wind god aspect of the Plumed Serpent.

Like Quetzalcóatl, Kukulcán had many other attributes as a creator, a god of new life and as a cultural hero who taught the ancestors skills such as farming in ancient times. In the Maya realms, his cult appears to have been an aristocratic one and he was particularly associated with lords and nobles. The cult of Kukulcán-Quetzalcóatl was very strong under the Toltecs, but temples in his honour were built much earlier at Teotihuacán and Tikal.

According to the Quiché Maya, the sky god was one of the two primal creators. He was associated with wind and rain, thunder and storms. The many names and identities he could adopt included Hurricane, Raw Thunderbolt and Newborn Thunderbolt. This associated him with the Aztec god Tezcatlipoca, who was also linked to hurricanes and rainstorms. The Aztec thunder god was Tláloc, bringer of rains.

Left: Éhecatl-Quetzalcóatl's breath brought the rains that fed the plants. Here the god carries five maize cobs on his back.

DELUGE: THE UNIVERSAL FLOOD

In both Aztec and Maya traditions there are myths of terrible destruction wrought by a great flood. According to the Quiché Maya, the failed creation of the wooden people was swept away by a universal flood sent by Huracán, who is associated with Tezcatlipoca. The Aztecs told that the fourth sun or world age was ended by a destructive flood sent by its ruling deity Chalchiúhtlicue, the goddess of oceans, lakes, rivers and streams.

THE WATERS UNLEASHED

In the version found in the late 16th-century *Codex Chimalpopoca*, one woman and one man were given the chance to survive the cataclysm in a story that is strikingly similar in some ways to the biblical narrative of Noah.

As the era reached its end, a man and woman named Nata and Nena were forewarned by the god Tezcatlipoca, who came to them and called them away from their activities. Nata was making the

Below: This image of a beast in floodwater was carved on a stone box that held the ashes of the Aztec tlatoani Ahuítzotl.

strong alcoholic drink *pulque*, but the god told him to put it aside and to go quickly to cut and hollow out a great cypress tree. In this makeshift boat Nata was to build a covered cabin in which to shelter from water, for at the end of the month of Tozoztli the waters that rise over the earth in the arc of the sky were going to be unleashed. The earth would be swamped. Just before this time, Nata and Nena should clamber into the cypress boat and wait. They should take with them just one ear of corn each and eat no more than that.

The couple did what they were told and they were thankful for, when the waters came, the flood submerged even the highest mountains in a single day. Death was everywhere, because there was no escaping from the water's awesome power.

Left: This intriguing stone lizard was carved by a Totonac craftsman in the period 1200–1300.

However, the two human survivors were soon hungry, for their corn was quickly gone. They clambered on to the roof of their makeshift cabin and looked around them. They realized that the great population of Mesoamerica had not been entirely wiped out for the people that Nata and Nena left behind had turned into fish, dolphins, whales and other sea creatures. The water was thick with marine life.

DISOBEDIENCE

Nata cried happily to his wife that they need not go hungry: the waters were teeming. They had a few sticks laid by in the cabin and with one of these Nata began to fish, while with some others Nena made a fire. Soon the smoke was rising in the sky and four meaty fish were roasting on the sticks above the fire. The sole human survivors ate them greedily, crying with joy that they had banished their hunger pains.

They did not look up to see that the smoke from their fire was rising to the thirteen layers of the heavens. Two gods – named in this source as Citlalícue and Citlatona – were angered by the smell and complained to Tezcatlipoca. He went quickly down to confront Nata and Nena, who had disobeyed his command that they should eat no more than one ear of corn each. He punished them for their greed. He took the fish Nata had caught and fashioned a long nose for their heads, with lithe legs and a tail for their hindquarters. The fish were transformed into dogs, which barked at the sky. They had no more escaped the flood than their fellows who had been transformed into fish. The flood lasted for a total of 52 years before the creation of the new world by Tezcatlipoca and his divine ally-rival the Plumed Serpent.

FISH, FLOODS AND FERTILITY

The Aztecs associated fish and waters with fertility. Fish were linked with the deities Chalchiúhtlicue, Xochiquetzal, Xochipilli, Mayáhuel, Quetzalcóatl and Cipactli. Fish from the lakes of Mexico were a staple food for the Aztecs. The majority of the offerings that have been found at the Great Pyramid in Tenochtitlán contained fish, but curiously there are few surviving representations of fish in Aztec art.

Below: Images of Tláloc's consort Chalchiúhtlicue often show her kneeling and wearing long ear tassels.

In view of its watery setting, the lake-city of Tenochtitlán must always have been vulnerable to flooding. The Spanish chronicler Diego Durán describes in his *History of the Indies of New Spain* describes how the *tlatoani* Ahuítzotl, his priests and people would perform obsequious offerings to the water goddess Chalchiúhtlicue in order to drive back a flood.

Left: The Aztecs removed masks such as this from Teotihuacán and used them as offerings at the Great Pyramid. This ritual mask may once have formed part of an incense burner used in religious ceremonies.

THE UNIVERSAL FLOOD: A RACE MEMORY?

Myths of a destructive universal flood are common in the traditions of diverse peoples across the world. In the Judaeo-Christian tradition there is the familiar tale of Noah, in which God sends a flood but saves Noah and his ark of animals and that of Gilgamesh in ancient Sumer.

Hindu religious mythology describes cycles of destruction and new life and tells how the universal waters cover the earth at the end of each age, before a new creation begins.

In Australia, the Worora aboriginals said that ancestral spirits once sent a vast flood to make space for the current world.

At the other end of the Earth, in the Arctic, the Inuit report that a previous world age knew no death, so that the world became dangerously overcrowded until a great flood swept the majority of people away, leaving a sustainable number, who were thereafter subject to death.

The myths are so common that some scholars have speculated there may once have been a great flood that brought near-universal destruction and that the memory of this cataclysm, buried deep in our subconscious, has inspired strikingly similar tales in cultures that have had no contact with one another.

However, in all likelihood the stories arose because flooding – whether by rivers and lakes or by the sea breaking through dykes and defensive walls – was common in so many places. Floodwaters brought death but also fertility. In the mythological imagination of early peoples, they became associated with the end of eras and the commencement of a new creation.

CHAPTER THREE

TALES OF THE GODS

In considering their gods, Mesoamericans were happy to combine the concepts of 'many' and 'one'. The Quiché Maya creators Huracán and Gucumatz were each both an individual and also a group of cooperating gods. The Aztecs simultaneously believed in many gods and one god. They knew of Ometeotl, the primeval god and first cause of creation. The god was both male and female, taking the forms Ometecuhtli and Omecihuatl. They were mother and father deities, seen as the creative essence of the primeval god.

In general the primeval deity was inactive in his own guise: other gods issued from Ometeotl through Ometecuhtli and Omecihuatl and were engaged in action. One story tells that Omecihuatl was wandering above the dry plains of the north, and felt a movement within her like the turning of a child in a woman's womb. She squatted there to give birth: a sacrificial knife of obsidian emerged from her, fell to the plain below and gave issue to 1,600 gods and goddesses. The number 1,600 is intended to mean 'beyond counting' – and suggests the myth confirms both the primacy of sacrifice and of the multiplicity of the gods. And just as the gods coexisted as 'one' and 'many', so each individual deity could take many forms without losing his or her essential identity. The ancient god Quetzalcóatl, for instance, could be known as the celebrated Plumed Serpent, the princely priest Topiltzin, the wind god Éhecatl and the planet Venus, among many other forms.

Left: A temple to the Plumed Serpent stood in the revered city of Teotihuacán. This image of the god greeted worshippers.

A CROWDED PANTHEON

The Aztecs' primeval deity, Ometeotl, does not appear to have been carved or otherwise represented: although one surviving Aztec sculpture *c.*1350 showing a seated god has been identified by some scholars as an image of the primeval god, other historians consider it to be Quetzalcóatl or the old god Huehuetéotl. The Aztecs did produce images of Ometeotl's constituent parts, Ometecuhtli/Tonacatecuhtli and Omecihuatl/Tonacacihuatl. They were often given rich clothes, perhaps intended to associate them with light.

GOD OF TWO FACES

Artists and craftsman also made more abstract attempts to represent the primeval deities. As early as the 8th century BC Mesoamericans produced intriguing two-faced or twin-headed figures thought by historians to represent the force of duality that was strongly present in the culture. The idea of duality, which holds opposites such as life/death or wet/dry in equilibrium, takes solid form in mythology in

Right: This Zapotec idol is of the goddess of the thirteen serpents, perhaps a version of the Aztec fertility goddess Cihuacóatl.

two-as-one deities such as Ometecuhtli/ Omecihuatl. Two-faced statues dating to this era have been found at Tlatilco. Scholars cite an Aztec mask that is half bare and half covered in skin as another representation of the same concept.

The Maya also believed in a creator deity, called Itzamná or Hunab Ku. In one version of the creation, Hunab Ku made the world three times: the first world contained dwarfs; the second contained a mysterious race called 'the offenders'; the third was the world of our era, inhabited by the Maya and their Aztec neighbours. Each of the first two creations was wiped out by a deluge and our own third age, too, was destined to end in the destruction of a universal flood. Sometimes Hunab Ku was seen, like Ometeotl, to be largely inactive in his own guise – but at the same time he was understood to be the father of Itzamná, who was moon god and bringer of culture to the people.

SERPENT IMAGERY

Itzamná taught the Maya how to write and use the sacred calendar, and he brought them knowledge of the maize and cacao plants.

As bringer of writing, Itzamná was the patron of scribes and priests. He is shown as a scribe in several illustrations to the *Madrid Codex*. He is usually shown as an old man seated on a throne, with a lined forehead and hollow cheeks, and because he was the moon god his headdress or forehead carries the glyph for night. He was also connected with new life, and linked to the snail – which was associated with childbirth. But his principal animal form was the serpent or dragon. A carved bone discovered in a tomb at Tikal shows a scribe's hand emerging from the mouth of a dragon that represents Itzamná.

Itzamná's consort was Ix Chel, the moon goddess. They were the parents of the bacabs, the giants who supported the heavens, separating earth and sky, in the four corners of creation.

Left: Carved snakes' heads guarded the steps of the pyramid temples at Tenochtitlán.

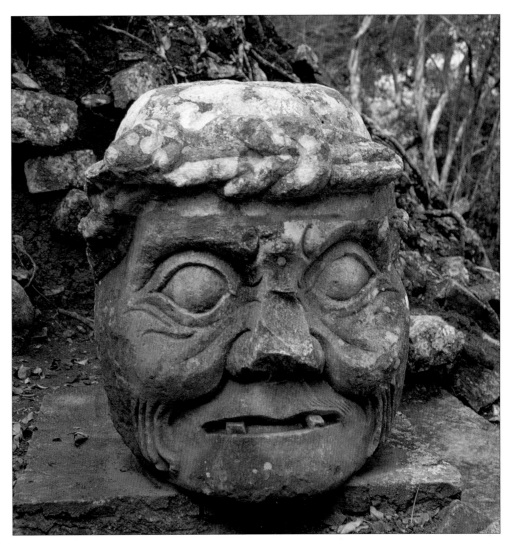

The prevalence of serpent imagery among the attributes and associations of quite different gods is suggestive of the fact that many of the deities were very closely connected, almost interchangeable. Mesoamericans believed that the divine essence was fluid and that it could take many associated forms. For the Classic-era Maya, Itzamná was linked to the serpent, and his consort Ix Chel was often shown with a snake hair-band. Itzamná was considered to be a creator, as was the sea god Sovereign Plumed Serpent by the Quiché Maya of the *Popol Vuh*.

The snake was also associated with spirit journeys and religious experience. The Maya developed the notion of the vision serpent, along whose coils the individual could travel to the spirit world or within which humans could encounter the gods. In Aztec carvings and art the open mouth of the serpent represents the cave Mesoamericans widely understood to be an entrance to the spirit world or to the underworld Mictlán.

Below: The Maya god Ix Chel was often depicted as a clawed goddess with a writhing serpent on her head and embroidered crossbones on her skirt.

The Aztecs (and the Toltecs before them) worshipped the snake in the form of the bird-serpent Quetzalcóatl, but the Aztecs also considered the earth goddess Coatlícue to have snake petticoats. The earth and sky were made from the dismembered body of a serpentine monster: sometimes the top layer of the earth was said to be composed of a carpet of interconnected serpents from which men, plants and animals had grown; the double-headed serpent represented in Aztec jewellery and art stood for the sky. One version of the myth of Topiltzin-Quetzalcóatl told how the god departed Mexico on a raft made of serpents.

Huitzilopochtli, sun deity and the Aztecs' tribal god, wielded a weapon called the *xiuhcóatl* or fire-snake to kill his countless brothers in the moments after his birth. In his form as Tonatiuh, the sun was led across the sky by the *xiuhcóatl* and by night fought in the underworld using the fire-snake as a weapon.

Above: This large carved head at the Maya city of Copán is thought to represent the god Itzamná, culture-giver and scribes' patron.

In one celebrated carving of Coatlícue, snakes represent the flow of blood from her cut arms and head. A sacrificial stone found in the Gulf of Mexico coastal region in the 19th century was carved in the shape of a two-headed snake, with a raised back on which the victim was pressed down while his heart was carved from his chest. Carvings of snakes-heads are known to have decorated the stairs on the Great Pyramid in Tenochtitlán.

Tláloc the rain and thunder god had a snake mask and was often depicted carrying a snake sceptre – driving rain was sometimes seen as a storm of water-snakes. In both Mesoamerican mythology and religion, the serpent was associated with the sun's rays, with rain, fertility and the earth, skill and power, the waters of the sea, human sexuality and rebirth.

49

LORD OF THE SMOKING MIRROR

Tezcatlipoca, the god of fate and bringer of discord and vice, was likened by Bernardino de Sahagún to the Christian devil. Tezcatlipoca had great powers and creative aspects but often put them to negative use, just like the angel Lucifer in the Christian tradition. Tezcatlipoca was a creator deity and shared the credit with Quetzalcóatl for the creation of the world from the body of the Earth Monster. However, whereas Quetzalcóatl was a civilizing cultural hero who introduced mankind to maize, Tezcatlipoca was a god of war who brought men into a cycle of destruction and new creation.

THE CULT OF TEZCATLIPOCA

Tezcatlipoca's cult went back at least as far as the Toltecs. They told a tale of a mirror of dark obsidian glass that could predict famine. At a time of great need, when people were starving in the land, Tezcatlipoca found and hid this mirror in order to prolong the people's suffering.

Left: This Tezcatlipoca mask was probably worn on a priest's waist. It was made from the front of a human skull.

The 'Lord of the Smoking Mirror', Tezcatlipoca, was believed to wear a mirror of the volcanic glass obsidian in the back of his head. Sometimes he was also said to have a mirror in place of one of his feet. Traditions vary as to whether Tezcatlipoca lost his foot when he and Quetzalcóatl were fighting the Earth Monster in order to create the earth and sky, or when he was flung out of the thirteenth heaven as punishment for misusing his dark power to seduce a fair goddess. Often he was depicted simply with a missing foot, his leg ending in the shinbone.

The glass he wore was said to be a 'smoking mirror' because it was made of obsidian, which characteristically gives a distorted reflection that is coloured green, grey or golden depending on the type used. Sometimes the glass was said to reflect the night even in full day; obsidian was linked in the Aztec imagination with cold and with the night, as was Tezcatlipoca himself. It was also associated with death and with the rain of windblown knives that travellers to the underworld of Mictlán had to pass through. According to the Franciscan friar Diego Durán, the author of *The History of the Indies of New Spain*, there was a religious statue made wholly of obsidian in the Templo Mayor or the sacred precinct in Tenochtitlán.

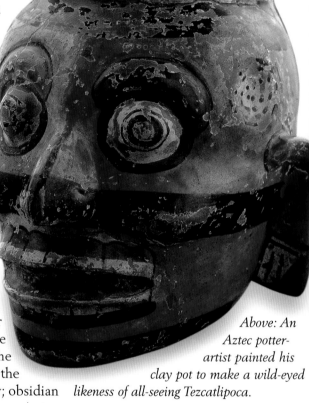

Above: An Aztec potter-artist painted his clay pot to make a wild-eyed likeness of all-seeing Tezcatlipoca.

The statue held a golden mirror. Using his shadowy mirror, Tezcatlipoca could see the patterns of the future and the private imaginings of people's hearts.

REFLECTING THE DARK SIDE

As the god of night, Tezcatlipoca was patron of hidden nocturnal activities, often shameful or wicked ones such as adultery and stealing. Sometimes he was depicted carrying a *tlachialoni*, a sceptre concealing a hole through which he could see the hidden side of people and their motives. The smoking mirror gave him access to the dark side, not only of people but also of the wider creation. He had within his control the forces of destruction as well as those of creation.

Above: The jaguar, a fierce aspect of Tezcatlipoca, was viewed with religious awe in Mesoamerica. These ravening cats are part of a mural from Teotihuacán.

DEATH EVERYWHERE

Tezcatlipoca was everywhere, invisible yet ubiquitous. Like the cold night sky, he was found in the north, south, east and west, although north was his particular direction. He resided in all the levels of the universe at once, even the underworld. He was also a god of the air, and of violent tempests, particularly hurricanes: he was associated with the Maya god Tahil.

Tezcatlipoca was also the coming destruction, for he would unleash the inevitable cataclysm destined to wipe away the current creation.

Tezcatlipoca was said to carry a sacrificial knife made of obsidian that symbolized a black wind devoid of life. Sacrificial knives were found in many of the offerings uncovered by archaeologists at the Templo Mayor in Tenochtitlán. In many, the knives are inserted into the nose or mouth of a skull mask. This symbolized the black wind that delivers death by stopping the flow of air, in contrast to the bright wind that is the breath of life.

LIFE AFTER CONQUEST

Obsidian, the volcanic glass associated so widely with Tezcatlipoca, was used by Spanish priests in a way that may have given Aztec onlookers secret amusement or satisfaction.

Archaeologists and historians have uncovered a number of obsidian blocks set in wood dating from the post-Conquest colonial period. Some are carved with Christian symbolism. Although some were doubtless used as mirrors, scholars believe that others were put to use as portable altars by travelling priests. To an Aztec, the 'smoking glass' obsidian would at once have suggested Tezcatlipoca. The god's association with shamanism, sorcery and treachery made his glass an unlikely material for priests to use for celebrating Mass. The great majority of the priests were probably ignorant of this powerful hidden association.

THE ORIGINATOR OF WAR

Alongside Huitzilopochtli, Tezcatlipoca was one of the Aztecs' principal warrior gods. A round shield called the *chimalli*, which was a symbol for battle conflict, was one of his accoutrements. In his human form, Tezcatlipoca was as youthful, virile and energetic as any eagle or jaguar warrior. The sacrifice of young victims at

Below: The Maya also worshipped the underworld jaguar god. This image is from the Temple of the Jaguar at Tikal.

the year's end granted the god eternal youthfulness. In this guise Tezcatlipoca was sometimes known as Telpochtli ('Young Warrior') and worshipped by a band of young devotees called the *telpochtiliztli*. A splendid funerary urn probably containing the ashes of a great warrior was found in the Templo Mayor in Tenochtitlán during excavations in 1978–82. It depicts Tezcatlipoca as a young warrior, carrying spears and an *atálatl* spear-thrower, wearing an

Above: In this image from the Codex Cospi *(c.1350–1500), Tezcatlipoca is in his black aspect, linked to the north and to death.*

eagle-feather headdress and spearhead nose-ring. In the Aztec codices he is also usually depicted as a soldier, carrying an *atlatl*, shield and darts and wearing two heron feathers in his hair to signify his status among the most elite groups of knights. His body is often painted black.

YÁOTL, THE ENEMY

Tezcatlipoca was the bringer of war, always at work stirring up conflict. In this guise, he was known as Yáotl ('the Enemy'). His presence was felt on the battlefield, although not as a protector. He presided over the give and take of war and decided when warriors should succeed and when they should fall. On his jacket were the skull and crossbones.

Tezcatlipoca loved and desired conflict for its own sake, but there was a positive side-effect to his stirring of wars, for on the battlefield the Aztecs gathered prisoners to carry home for sacrifice in the sacred precinct in Tenochtitlán. In this sense, his promotion of war was less a malign activity and more a valuable contribution to the religious cycle of sacrifice.

Above: This codex image depicts the dark lord Tezcatlipoca as a virile warrior, equipped with shield and weapon.

Above: An image from Bernardino de Sahagún's Florentine Codex *(1575–7) shows a sacrifice in honour of Tezcatlipoca.*

ANIMAL FORMS

All Aztec gods had one or more animal forms. Tezcatlipoca was associated particularly with the jaguar, which was like the god in that it was fierce, unpredictable and favoured the night.

The Lord of the Smoking Mirror was believed to roam the earth in the dark hours, sometimes in the form of this stealthy, keen-visioned predator. As the jaguar, Tezcatlipoca was associated with the sun during its night-time passage through the dangerous regions of the underworld. In one version of the myth describing the end of the current creation, it is told how, in that era, Tezcatlipoca would steal the sun, so bringing the world, gods and men to black nothingness.

Among his other animal forms were the deceitful skunk, the mischievous monkey and the sly coyote. Aztecs thought the coyote had particular sexual potency and Tezcatlipoca's association with him was located in the god's aspect as a deity of masculinity.

NEGATIVE AND POSITIVE POWER

Tezcatlipoca had many other attributes, always combining negative and positive aspects. His connection to the night and to the jaguar made him god of sorcerer-shamans. He was said to be 'the Left-handed One', suggesting that he was never to be trusted and that he would come at men unexpectedly. He was understood to be mocking mankind, binding them with evil. If a man or woman endured great humiliation it was understood by all to be the work of Tezcatlipoca.

Tezcatlipoca was also associated with rulers and kingly qualities; the coronation preparations of the Aztec *tlatoani* included rites in Tezcatlipoca's honour. According to one tradition, it was Tezcatlipoca, alongside Huitzilopochtli, who guided the México/Aztecs on their journey to find a place to settle. He is said to have inspired the travelling tribe by recounting the marvellous vision of their future riches and dominance that he could see in his shadow-mirror.

Some of the priests of Tenochtitlán painted their bodies black in honour of Tezcatlipoca, using a dark paste made from ground mushrooms, snake skin and tobacco. Tezcatlipoca helped the Aztecs in their divinely ordained mission to provide blood nourishment for the gods. The religious festival of Tóxcatl in May, when a youthful representative of Tezcatlipoca was sacrificed in the dark lord's honour, was one of the major festivals of the Aztec year. As the youth was led to sacrifice up the temple steps, the earthly form of Tezcatlipoca would play mournfully on a thin flute that was carved in the likeness of a flower at its end.

Tezcatlipoca's feast day was 1-Death in the sixth thirteen-day 'month' of the 260-day calendar. At the festival of Teotleco (Coming of the Gods and Goddesses), a bowl of maize flour was laid in the temple and a night vigil was kept until a footprint in the bowl was hailed as the sign that the gods had come. According to some accounts, this footprint was understood to be that of Tezcatlipoca, leading the main group of gods and goddesses. He was not the first to arrive, however. This was always the youngest and fastest god, Tlamatzincatl.

DARK CHALLENGER BY NIGHT

Tezcatlipoca was a constant danger by night. A man out alone on night roads might expect to be challenged by the dark god, who was believed to roam the country looking for victims. If Tezcatlipoca met a traveller, he would challenge him to a bout of wrestling. A mortal who defeated the god could ask for anything he pleased and know that it would be granted. In this guise, Tezcatlipoca was associated with the night wind. Stone benches were built alongside the more important roadways to provide a resting place for this most unpredictable of gods;

Below: Tezcatlipoca's reputation for virility associated him with the coyote, believed by Aztecs to be sexually powerful.

Above: An unknown deity emerges from the mouth of the divine jaguar in a terracotta piece from the Zapotec city of Monte Albán.

unfortunately he often used these as sites for his ambushes. Some nights he sent thieves to do his work for him.

DANGEROUS ENERGY
A body of myths recounted how Tezcatlipoca's dangerous energy caused havoc among the Toltec people of Tollán at the time when the priest Topiltzin-Quetzalcóatl was at the height of his powers there. Tezcatlipoca travelled there to cause trouble, scantily clad with his almost naked body painted green, posing as a salesman of green paint. He knew that Huemac, who served Quetzalcóatl by governing Tollán, had a daughter whose beauty was the talk of the whole Valley of Mexico, for her appearance was more wonderful even than that of Mount

Ixtaccíhuatl. Many Toltecs longed to marry her. Tezcatlipoca made sure that he passed close to her bedchamber for he hoped to arouse strong desires in her soul. His plan worked, as he knew it would.

The princess saw the vigorous body and bright flashing eyes of the wandering salesman and fell deeply in love. She took to her bed, pining for love, and her father became worried. When he asked her handmaidens what the matter was, they explained that a passing stranger had undone his daughter, arousing passions in her that would give her no rest. Huemac summoned the

Below: An enigmatic Aztec figure (c.1200–1500) combines the features of the living (right) and the fleshless dead (left).

stranger to his court and asked him his business. Tezcatlipoca was casual. He explained that he went almost naked because it was the custom where he came from and said that his life was not of great importance to him. The king could kill him, if he pleased, to punish him for stealing his daughter's heart. However, Huemac knew that if he sacrificed the young man it would be the death of his lovelorn daughter, so instead he commanded the handsome stranger to marry the beautiful princess.

This caused great upset among the people of Tollán, but the king launched a war in order to distract them.

Tezcatlipoca went unannounced among the troops, but some soldiers recognized him as the stranger who had stolen the princess from them. They tricked him into occupying a vulnerable position on the battlefield, where they hoped he would be slain. When the moment came, however, he fought with the greatest valour and won a fine reputation.

A DEADLY DANCE

Back in Tollán, Tezcatlipoca was the toast of the city. He could do no wrong and was cheered wherever he went, attired in warrior's garb, with his beautiful wife on his arm. Now he unleashed the full force of his power on the unsuspecting people. He announced that there would be a public feast and celebration and at the appointed time the Toltecs crowded enthusiastically into the main plaza. Then he began to sing and made the people dance to his song. Faster he sang, and faster, and the people had to fling themselves into the

steps to stay ahead of the music. Faster still and faster he sang, until the dance was unbearable for the assembled crowd.

The people could no longer keep their footing, and they fell helplessly into a ravine that the god had made in the solid earth. They tumbled down the steep sides like so many rocks. It was over – they were dead.

A GOD AVENGES HIS OWN DEATH

Another tale told how Tezcatlipoca invited all the people of Tollán to meet him in the city's fair flower gardens. He hid himself in the shade, then leapt out on his victims, killing many with a simple hoe, while others fled in panic, trampling one another. Many hundreds of innocents died.

Another story told how Tezcatlipoca punished the Toltecs for his own death. He was again entertaining the people in the main plaza, this time by displaying a child dancing in his hand, who was in truth, the warlike Aztec deity Huitzilopochtli. By using fantastic magic Tezcatlipoca made the child appear to dance on his outstretched palm. The people crowded urgently around, creating such a crush that many people were killed. This unleashed the fury of the survivors and they turned on the gods Tezcatlipoca and Huitzilopochtli, pummelling them until they died.

The gods' death was not the end of the affair. Their corpses began to leak a hideous-smelling liquid and gave off a gas so foul that any who smelled it died instantly. A few came in masks to drag the pestilential corpses away, but they found that the divine bodies were far too heavy to shift. They tied them up with strong cords and gathered a huge crowd to pull, but the ropes broke and the people tumbled in a great heap, one suffocating the next. In the end the entire population died.

Left: This elaborate funerary urn was found in Teotihuacán, revered by the Aztecs as perhaps the site of the Tollán of myth.

THE PLUMED SERPENT

Quetzalcóatl's name has two meanings. In itself, it comprises two Nahuatl words, each of which also has two meanings. *Quetzal* can mean 'green feather' or 'precious' and *cóatl* can mean 'serpent' or 'twin'. The elements of the name taken together can therefore mean 'Plumed Serpent' or 'Precious Twin'. Each name evokes an aspect or role played by Quetzalcóatl in the Mesoamerican pantheon. Such dual meaning also

Below: A 4th-century homage to the Plumed Serpent is suggestive of the god's possible origins in an ancient dragon deity.

demonstrates the concept of duality so characteristic of Mesoamerican deities and religion in general.

A HUMAN AVATAR

Quetzalcóatl was the only one of the Aztec gods to have had a human avatar in the person of Topiltzin, the priestly ruler of Tollán. In addition, because of his association with wise governance and kingly qualities, many earthly rulers took his name and wore the green feathers of his animal familiar, the quetzal bird. These rulers may have been understood to be representatives of the god on Earth. Quetzalcóatl was a protector of rulers and their families. He was also a great cultural hero, inventor of the ritual calendar, teacher of farming skills and protector of craftsmen. In the form of an ant, he was responsible for bringing the maize plant to humans.

TWIN FORMS

God and man, man and serpent, the 'Precious Twin' was a god of duality; of twin forms. His cult goes far back into Mesoamerican history. The oldest

Above: This magnificent double-headed serpent pectoral may have been part of the treasure sent to Cortés by Moctezuma II.

surviving image of Quetzalcóatl, found at Tlatilco, dates to *c.*800BC, while a pyramid temple to the god was built at Teotihuacán in the 3rd century AD. His cult probably grew from that of an ancient Mesoamerican sky god, a dragon who was also worshipped as a fertility and agricultural deity because of his ability to deliver fresh winds and life-giving rains. However, he was also seen as a god of land-level waters – in the *Popol Vuh* the Plumed Serpent is the sea god – and among his myriad attributes he had the power to unleash floods. When the Spanish conquistadors came to Cholula, the priests there tried to provoke the anger of Quetzalcóatl as god of the waters. They encouraged the invaders to desecrate the temple of the Plumed Serpent in the hope that the god would send a flood to drive the Europeans back. However, the plan misfired because Quetzalcóatl did not respond to their insults.

CONNECTIONS TO FERTILITY

The Plumed Serpent's connections to fertility were made clear in one Aztec myth of his conception and birth. According to this tale, Quetzalcóatl was the daughter of Cihuacóatl, a fertility and earth goddess whose name means 'Woman Serpent'. Cihuacóatl often took the shape of a deer. In early times, long before the México travelled south from the northern steppes in which they originated, she roamed the earth as a two-headed deer. In this form she attracted the attention of the hunting god Mixcóatl ('Cloud Serpent'), who pursued her through steep valleys and across wide plains, and all along the shores of the lakes, until he had her in his sights. With one well-aimed dart he brought her low. However, in that same instant he also lost her, for before his eyes the beast transformed into a woman of surpassing beauty. Now the hunt was on again. Mixcóatl pursued this maiden across the landscape until he caught her. Then they had sexual relations. The fruit of their lovemaking was the Plumed Serpent Quetzalcóatl.

Quetzalcóatl was also associated with a range of attributes and natural states that were in opposition to those of his ancient rival and foe Tezcatlipoca. Tezcatlipoca was associated with night, deception and cycles of violence, whereas Quetzalcóatl was linked to daylight, clear thinking and a good life. Both gods were associated with the winds, but while Tezcatlipoca was the god of night winds and hurricanes, Quetzalcóatl-Éhecatl was lord of the morning winds that bring light to the fields. Some scholars understand the ancient image of the sky serpent – often represented with its tail in its mouth – as a homage to the sun, and Quetzalcóatl had some connection to the Earth's star. Indeed, many Aztec gods had solar aspects.

Priests of Quetzalcóatl wore a conch shell whose patterning represented the movement of the wind and honoured the

Left: Some 14cm (6in) tall, this shell-mosaic piece dates from the Toltec period and may once have graced a palace in Tula.

Above: Another view of the shell-mosaic piece of Quetzalcóatl, in human form. Bursting forth from the jaws of a coyote, he represents life springing from the Earth.

god in his guise as the wind god Éhecatl. Quetzalcóatl was particularly associated with the priesthood and he was regarded as the protector of the priestly school in Tenochtitlán. The two foremost members of the priestly hierarchy were called 'Quetzalcóatl' as part of their title, despite the fact that they presided over the worship of other gods.

In his guise as a priestly patron, Quetzalcóatl was represented as a man with skin painted black and a long beard. In this role and in his form as the wind god, Éhecatl, Quetzalcóatl is often shown wearing a conical hat. The Maya of Yucatán worshipped the Plumed Serpent as Kukulcán, god of wind, light and waters with some solar characteristics. Among the Maya he was particularly revered as a thunder god.

QUETZALCÓATL AND THE RAFT OF SNAKES

Many myths tell of Quetzalcóatl's enduring conflict with the dark lord Tezcatlipoca. In his guise as the historical-mythical Toltec ruler Topiltzin, Quetzalcóatl was decisively defeated by his opponent and forced to leave the city of Tollán. So ended a golden era of peace and wonderful artistic achievement. There are various versions of his downfall, but according to one, the formerly pure-minded priest-king was tricked by Tezcatlipoca into becoming drunk on the strong liquor known as *pulque* and disgraced himself by seducing his own sister. He left in shame.

Topiltzin-Quetzalcóatl determined to sacrifice himself as a mark of his penitence. He dressed himself in his purest finery, including the kingly mask of turquoise, and built a pyre of great tree-trunks. Then he stepped on to the bonfire and lit it himself. He did not flinch at the touch of fire, just as the god Nanahuatzin, who became the sun, went

Below: A figurine from Teotihuacán shows Quetzalcóatl in human form but with a serpent's divided tongue.

unflinching into the flames. The flames roared. In an instant, all the king's finery and his royal body were ash. His soul became a spark that rose to the sky and settled in the form of Venus, the morning star. In this guise, Quetzalcóatl was known as Ce Ácatl or Tlahuizcalpantecuhtli: he was a malign force, the enemy of the sun. He was also feared and revered – in the form of Xólotl – as Venus the evening star.

THE END OF TOLLÁN

Another version of the myth describes how Topiltzin-Quetzalcóatl left the city, made a penitential procession to the seacoast and departed on a raft made of snakes, bound for the land of Tlapallán, whence he had originally come. First he burned the splendid buildings of Tollán, then buried the great treasures and artworks for which his reign was famous in the deep mountain valleys nearby. He transformed the cacao trees that had grown in the city into mesquites and commanded the beautiful bird that had graced Tollán to depart a great distance. Tollán was bereft of its leader and of its beauty. An era had ended.

Topiltzin-Quetzalcóatl departed, with a troop of palace assistants and pages following in his footsteps. After some hours of walking and exhausted by grief, he stopped at a place called Quauhtitlán. He asked his assistant to hand him a mirror and, examining his reflection, sighed deeply. 'I am old,' he said quietly, and handed the mirror back to his assistant. The pages were weeping, because of the king's inexplicable wrongdoing and

Above: This turquoise and shell mask has holes in the eyes to allow the wearer to see and was probably worn by a priest.

because they understood that, in this time-bound physical world, what is perfect and true, like the era of Topiltzin-Quetzalcóatl's rule in Tollán, cannot endure for ever. The dark shadow of Tezcatlipoca is behind every beam of light. The place was ever afterwards known as Huehuequauhtitlán ('Old Quauhtitlán') because the king saw his aged face there and was saddened. They went on then, with one of the palace musicians playing a mournful air on the flute like the victim who impersonated Tezcatlipoca in the festival of Tóxcatl. When Topiltzin-Quetzalcóatl was too tired to go further, he sat on a roadside rock, again sighing deeply. The god-prince left the mark of his hands in this stone, and the place was afterwards known as Temacpalco ('The Imprint of Hands').

They went on again when Topiltzin-Quetzalcóatl was rested. At Coaapán they met a group of Aztec deities who asked the god-prince where he was going and for what reason. He replied that he was going back to his place of origin, Tlapallán, because his father the sun had called him home. The gods allowed him to pass, but demanded that Quetzalcóatl deliver the secrets of his divine magic; the supreme spells that lay behind the creation of the wonders of his rule in Tollán. Topiltzin-Quetzalcóatl refused and threw all his spells into the fountain named Cozcaapa.

The procession of penitents came to a high pass close to a volcano in the Sierra Nevada mountains. It was too cold in this forlorn spot for mere mortals and all of the palace followers died, leaving

Below: A 3rd-century BC bas-relief celebrates the life-giving force and regal power of the ancient Plumed Serpent.

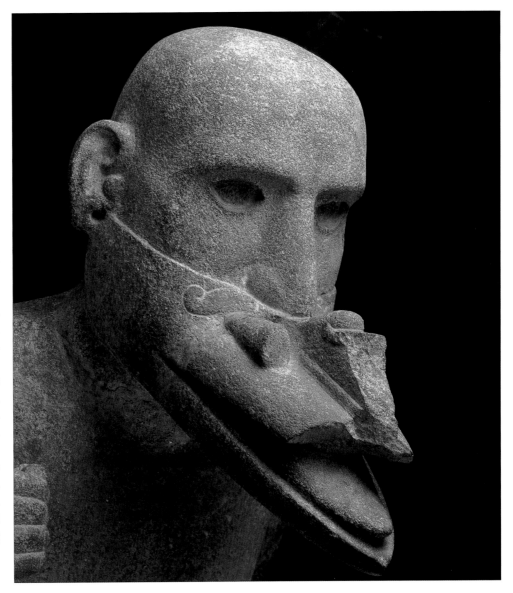

Above: This powerful statue of Quetzalcóatl in his guise as Éhecatl, lord of the winds, was found in Calixtlahuaca, Mexico.

Topiltzin-Quetzalcóatl to mourn them with singing and flute-playing of the most exquisite beauty. He climbed to the peak of Mount Poyauhtécatl, then went down to the far side by sliding. He came at last, and alone, to the shore of the Eastern Sea (which today is known as the Gulf of Mexico) and here summoned the snakes of the entire coastal region. From them he made a raft and then he threw the magical vessel made of snakes on to the waters. He departed for Tlapallán on his snake raft. Those who await his return know that he will come back in the same way, by sea, to found anew the glorious kingdom of Tollán.

It has often been suggested that Moctezuma believed Hernán Cortés to be the returning divinity Topiltzin-Quetzalcóatl and that it was for this reason he treated the Spanish conquistadors with reverence rather than

the suspicion they merited. It was a happy coincidence for the Spanish invaders that they arrived in the year 1-Reed, which had been prophesied as the year in which the god would return, and that the first encounter between Cortés and Moctezuma took place on Quetzalcóatl's name day. The *tlatoani* received a gift of wine and biscuits from Cortés, but refused them and sent them to be buried in the temple of Quetzalcóatl at Tollán in honour of the god 'whose sons have arrived'. According to Bernardino de Sahagún, when Moctezuma greeted Cortés with a splendid speech at the gates of Tenochtitlán, he declared that the arriving leader had come from the 'unknown…a place of mystery'.

THE TRIBAL WAR GOD

The Aztecs' patron god, deity of war and of the sun, was a fierce warrior from the first moment of his life. According to the myth of his birth, Huitzilopochtli came from his mother's womb fully armed. His mother was the earth goddess Coatlícue, who in one account also mothered Quetzalcóatl. Coatlícue was priestess of a shrine high on the mountain at Coatepec, near the Toltec capital of Tollán or Tula. One day, as she was cleaning the shrine, she saw a ball of brightly coloured feathers descend on to her breast. She thought little of it, but rather than discard the feathers she placed them in her belt. However, when she next looked she found out that the ball had disappeared and soon afterwards she discovered the feathers had miraculously made her pregnant.

A PROTECTIVE SON

Coatlícue's existing children included one daughter, the moon goddess Coyolxauhqui, and sons almost beyond counting, the Centzonhuitznahuac ('The Four Hundred Southerners'). When they saw their mother was pregnant they were angry, for they were suspicious of her claim that the pregnancy was a miracle and suspected that she had been

Below: The xiuhcóatl *or fire-serpent brandished by Huitzilopochtli forms the motif on this mosaic disc from Chichén Itzá.*

Above: Huitzilopochtli's mother Coatlícue represents the surface of the Earth and its power to bring life from the death of winter.

promiscuous. The children gathered at the foot of the mountain and Coyolxauhqui convinced her brothers to punish their mother by putting her to death. High above in her mountain shrine, Coatlícue heard their raised voices and knew what they were planning. She shivered with fear, but then heard a voice issuing from her womb: she must not be afraid, the voice said, for her new child would protect her.

When Coyolxauhqui and the Four Hundred Southerners arrived to launch their attack, Huitzilopochtli emerged to repel them. His skin was painted blue and he wore the body armour that would later be adopted by Aztec warriors. The bright feathers of the hummingbird – the same feathers that had fallen in a ball on to the chest of Coatlícue – covered his left leg. This justified his name of

'Hummingbird of the Left'. With the *xiuhcóatl* or fire-serpent he held in his hand, he cut Coyolxauhqui into many pieces. These fell down the mountainside and landed, all jumbled up, on the plain below. Then he killed his brothers, left and right, allowing a few bedraggled survivors to escape to the south.

VICTORY FOR THE SUN

The myth proclaims the primacy of the sun, represented by Huitzilopochtli, over his moon sister Coyolxauhqui. The weapon the sun god used was the fire-serpent which was believed to guide the sun across the sky by day. His mother is the serpent-skirted earth from which the sun appears to issue each dawn, and the Four Hundred Southerners are the southern stars of the night sky that are routed every morning as the light of the sun spreads far and wide.

This victory was commemorated in a celebrated sculpture of Coyolxauhqui's dismembered body that lay at the foot of the steps of the Great Pyramid in Tenochtitlán, where the bodies of sacrificial victims landed. The tale of sun and moon deities Huizilopochtli and Coyolxauhqui is therefore a variation on the myth of the creation of the sun and

Below: This sculpture of Coyolxauhqui's massacred body received the blood of many victims that poured off the Great Pyramid.

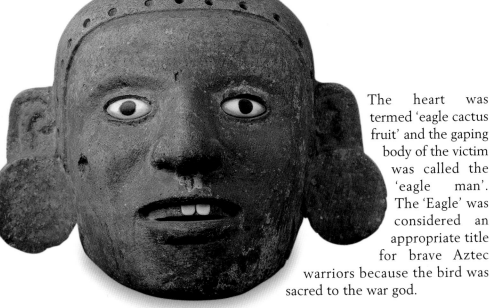

The heart was termed 'eagle cactus fruit' and the gaping body of the victim was called the 'eagle man'. The 'Eagle' was considered an appropriate title for brave Aztec warriors because the bird was sacred to the war god.

A surviving Aztec hymn to Huitzilopochtli praises him as a young warrior dressed in yellow feathers who makes the sun appear. It praises the god for moving the sun across the heavens and associates him with the god Nanahuatzin when it declares, 'Here he comes forward, one well dressed in paper, who lives in the place that burns.'

Below: The fire serpent is celebrated in this Aztec sculpture at Tenayuca.

Above: Made from stone, with shell eyes and obsidian for the eyeballs, this arresting mask evokes qualities of youthful vigour.

moon at Teotihuacán and of the enmity born there between the sun, Nanahuatzin and the moon, Tecuciztécatl. The story of Huitzilopochtli's birth also celebrates and establishes the Aztec tradition of martial vigour, conflict and bloodletting.

Spanish chroniclers have likened Huitzilopochtli to Hercules, the mythical Greek hero who performed twelve wondrous 'labours' or feats of strength and bravery. Huitzilopochtli was usually depicted wearing a plume of humming-bird feathers on his head, with his face, arms and legs painted with blue stripes. He carried four spears in one hand and a reed shield bearing five tufts of eagle's down on his other arm. The spears had eagle's down rather than the usual hard flint at their tips.

EAGLE IMAGERY
The eagle was principal among the creatures associated with the war and sun god, and eagle imagery played a major part in acts of ritual human sacrifice performed in Huitzilopochtli's honour in which the human heart was torn out. When the priest removed the heart from the victim's flayed chest, he held it up to the sun in triumphant dedication, then flung it into one of the *cuauhxicalli* ('eagle vessels') placed nearby.

HUMMINGBIRD OF THE LEFT

Huitzilopochtli, the Aztecs' war and sun god, had no antecedents among the deities of earlier Mesoamerican peoples. According to their own origin myths, Huitzilopochtli travelled south with the Méxica or Aztecs when they entered the Valley of Mexico from the less hospitable lands to the north. In some accounts he led the tribe on its migration, in others his idol was carried by a group of four priests and made several divine prophecies of their coming greatness.

DUALITY OF LIFE AND DEATH
The Aztecs took care to establish their god's standing alongside older Mesoamerican deities. At the top of the Great Pyramid in Tenochtitlán, a shrine to Huitzilopochtli stood along-side one to the rain god Tláloc, one of the oldest gods of the region. In Huitzilopochtli's temple a sacred flame burned that had to be kept alight at all costs. The Aztecs understood that if it were allowed to die then their power and ascendancy over the other peoples of the region would abruptly come to an end. Twin temples to a rain god and a war god symbolized the duality of life and death. It also symbolized the incompatible opposition of water and fire, which the Aztecs used as an image for war. The Great Pyramid in the sacred complex

Right: The god Huitzilopochtli's mother, Coatlícue, was believed to take the bodies of the dead.

at Tenochtitlán was intended as a recreation in stone of the hill of Coatepec ('Serpent Mountain'), where the tribal god was born, and of Mount Tonacatépetl, where the staple food maize was discovered, as well as of Mount Tláloc, the peak sacred to the rain god, on which important fertility and rain festivals were held.

Huitzilopochtli's own standing was further bolstered by the god's identification with south, the sacred direction of Blue Tezcatlipoca, one of the four creator-sons of the lord of duality Ometeotl.

HUMMINGBIRDS
Huitzilopochtli's name means 'Hummingbird of the Left'. Left was used in the Aztecs' Nahuatl tongue to refer to south, the region with which hummingbirds were associated. Hummingbirds were connected to blood sacrifice, for the blood let by the priest from his own body or that of a sacrificial victim was compared to the nectar drawn by a humming-bird from a flower. The birds also became connected to war. The souls of warriors killed in battle were said to take the form of hummingbirds and to accompany the sun in its climb each morning from the dawn horizon to its zenith.

Huitzilopochtli occupied a primary position in Aztec religious life. The festival of Panquetzalíztli ('Lifting of the

Above: Some authorities identify this highly polished obsidian mask as an image of Ixtilton, Huitzilopochtli's lieutenant.

Banners'), which was held in November and December in Huitzilopochtli's honour, was one of the most important of the Aztec year. Although none survives, we know from documentary evidence that major statues of Huitzilopochtli stood in the sacred precinct of Tenochtitlán and in the main religious areas of Texcoco and Tlatelolco.

LADY OF DISCORD
Huitzilopochtli was thirsty for human blood and many thousands of human victims were slain in his honour by the Aztecs. The majority were prisoners of the wars that the god promoted, but on occasion he demanded other victims.

CHAPTER FOUR

WATERS, FERTILITY AND HARVEST

In ancient times, long before the Aztecs worshipped their hummingbird war god Huitzilopochtli, Mesoamerican farmers made regular offerings to fertility and water gods hoping to secure frequent rains and a bumper harvest. Major gods of the Aztec period, such as the Plumed Serpent, Quetzalcóatl, and Lord of the Smoking Mirror, Tezcatlipoca, developed from primordial deities whose powers were primarily over rain, waters and the fertility of the land – sky gods with the power to deliver wet winds, storms, lightning and thunderbolts. The cult of the Aztec rain god Tláloc and the Maya rain god Chac can be traced back to the Olmec civilization at La Venta in 800BC.

In the Aztec era, worshippers at the *Templo Mayor* within the sacred precinct in Tenochtitlán brought varied offerings to many gods, especially Huitzilopochtli and Tláloc, whose temples had the prime positions at the top of the pyramid, closest to the sacred sky. But while the two gods shared centre stage in the imperial capital, in most areas – particularly in agricultural communities – worshippers felt more attached to the older cult of the rain god and his associated fertility deities than to the worship of Huitzilopochtli, patron of the war-driven Aztec state and empire.

Left: The Aztec cult of Xochiquetzal – goddess of beauty, love, flowers and the domestic arts – was one of many that grew from ancient Mesoamerican worship of fertility goddesses. This image of Xochiquetzal is from the Codex Vaticanus.

THE SACRIFICE OF BLOOD AND WATER

The cult of the rain god was crucial to Mesoamerican religion. In the *Codex Borgia*, for example, the Aztec universe is represented with five figures of Tláloc, Aztec god of rains; one stands in the east, one in the north, one in the south and one in the west, with a fifth in the centre. This cosmic map is comparable to other similar representations of the Earth divided into four quarters and a centre. In other versions of the map, each place is associated with a different god and also with a different one of the five suns or world ages. In the Borgia version, each of the Tláloc figures is standing on an image

Below: The temples of the ancient god Tláloc and the Aztec tribal deity Huitzilopochtli stand side by side at the Templo Mayor *in Tenochtitlán, in this fanciful print by Fumagalli.*

of the earth goddess suggesting that, in every place and in every age, the relationship between the fields and the clouds, the land and the sky, the earth and the rain, is of prime importance.

FERTILITY FOR THE EARTH

Even the demand for sacrificial human blood by Huitzilopochtli and other deities was driven by the desire to guarantee the fertility of the earth. The Aztecs equated blood and water: human blood was the precious liquid that sustained life as water was to the earth. This religious understanding was given symbolic form in sacrifices to the Aztec spring and vegetation god Xipe Totec, whose victims were often shot with arrows rather than despatched by another method of sacrifice. They were tied to frames and as the blood

Above: A priestly coat of shells must have made as much an audible impression as a visual impact during religious ceremonies.

flowed from their wounds it dripped on to a stone that symbolically stood for the thirsty earth, just as the rains fed new growth each spring for Xipe Totec. Similarly, the reclining *chacmool* figures on which priests placed the hearts of sacrificial victims were representations of Tláloc. The mask visible over the eyes and mouth on the *chacmools* identifies them as images of the rain god.

THE ENDING OF WATER

Tláloc was honoured with human blood sacrifice in the festival of Atlcahualo ('The Ending of Water'), which took place in the first month of the Aztec year (14 February–5 March in the Western calendar). Children and young people were sacrificed in his honour and that of his consort Chalchiúhtlicue. The rain god's cult was strongly associated with the fertility of the land. The importance of rain to farmers meant that priests of

Chalchiúhtlicue, piles of boulders represented the deities, who were associated with the mountaintops that appeared to summon the long-awaited rain-clouds.

ANNUAL PILGRIMAGE FOR WATER

One of the peaks visible from Tenochtitlán was named in Tláloc's honour and the rulers of the Valley's principal cities made an annual pilgrimage to a shrine on the mountain in the dry season of April and May. Offerings to Tláloc and Chalchiúhtlicue were regularly made in sacred caves high on the mountainsides. For example, a figure of Tláloc fashioned from sticks and covered in resin and copal was found in a cavern on the volcano Ixtaccíhuatl. Scholars believe that figures such as this would normally have been burned at the ends of the rituals and worshippers might have believed that the dark, holy smoke made by the resin and copal had the power to 'blacken' the clouds, turning windblown white travellers into dark clouds laden with rain.

NECESSARY EQUILIBRIUM

Tláloc did not always hold droughts at bay. The forces of dryness and wetness, rains and drought were balanced in a proper equilibrium. Blood sacrifices were necessary, not to propitiate the rain god or ease his anger, but to maintain this equilibrium. An intriguing greenstone figure discovered at Tlatilco and dating to *c.*1500 appears to be a three-dimensional representation of this concept. The figure's face is divided in two down the middle: one half wears the distinctive 'goggles' of Tláloc and has that god's snake-fang

Above: Images of Xipe Totec, the god presiding over the germination of seeds, often show him with a crenellated headdress.

mouth, while the other suggests a smooth-faced young man, thought to represent drought. Together the two halves suggest the proper balance of the seasons in the Mesoamerican farming year. So long as the balance of the seasons held, all was well. If calamity struck it was not because part of the year was dry but because the drought did not end; because the equilibrium had been disturbed. Sacrifice was needed to maintain the flow of divine energy in the cosmos.

Above: Water goddess Chalchiúhtlicue is missing her face and hands because she was deliberately damaged by zealous Spaniards.

Tláloc played a crucial role in agricultural and fertility festivals such as Ochpaniztli ('Clearing'), which took place in September. The priests would make obeisances before Tláloc's image while wearing an elaborate costume. This included a Tláloc serpent mask and a cone-shaped headdress decorated with bark paper strips, a snake sceptre and a bag of copal.

Tláloc's name derives from Nahuatl *tlalli* ('the earth') and *oc,* used as a suffix to denote something settling above or on the surface of an object. At the start of the rainy season clouds collected above the surface of the earth, rising from the canyons and floating up to jostle one another in the thin air around the mountain peaks. At shrines to Tláloc and

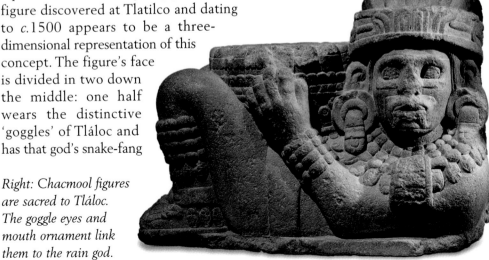

Right: Chacmool figures are sacred to Tláloc. The goggle eyes and mouth ornament link them to the rain god.

ANCIENT LIFEGIVERS

Worship of the rain god probably went back to the dawn of Mesoamerican civilization. From the earliest settlements, farmers feared the long and harsh droughts that periodically afflicted the region, bringing humankind's best efforts to nothing. They fervently worshipped the rain god to bring the end of drought and to provide lush crops. He was revered under various names by different peoples and in different periods. To the Maya he was Chac; to the Zapotecs he was Cocijo; to the Totonacs he was Tajín and to the Aztecs he was Tláloc. He was generally regarded as chief of the fertility gods, with dominion over lesser deities of the fields, flowers and crops, including maize.

FOUR GREAT JARS

Like many Aztec gods, Tláloc had a dual nature, bringing both good and bad. He could deliver drought and frosts as well as fertilizing downpours and brought welcome and unwelcome forms of rain – the gentler rains that fed the land and the torrential storms that made the lands flood and spoiled the crops where they stood in the fields. He governed lightning strikes and could also send disease. The Aztecs believed that Tláloc had four great jars, one for each of the four cardinal points. From the jar of the east he brought fruitful rains to Mesoamerica but from the others he unleashed disease, freezing conditions and drought.

The Aztecs also believed that Tláloc stored rainwater in the mountains that towered over the Valley of Mexico and that he was the god of running waters in the mountains. One myth tells how he sends his helpers, the *tlaloques*, to collect water from the mountains in sacred vessels. With their way cleared by the wind god Éhecatl-Quetzalcóatl, they carry the water to the vault of the sky where it forms into rain-bearing clouds.

The *tlaloques* could bring five types of rain. In addition to life-giving rain to nourish the crops, they also brought

Above: This figure of the Aztec rain god Tláloc wears the very large ear decorations usually associated with the god.

unwanted storms whose winds and lashing rains flattened plants, fungal rain that caused diseases in the maize, flint rain (probably hail or hard driving rain) that pummelled plants, and fire rain, which probably referred to the rain that accompanies lightning storms or to the absence of rain in times of drought.

The serpent imagery, so important in Mesoamerica, was powerfully connected to fertility and was central to the cult of Tláloc. The god's face was often depicted made of snakes, with two curled

Right: A figurine of the Maya rain god Chac has the god's characteristic prominent nose.

serpents representing the eyes and joining in the centre as the nose and a snake 'moustache' above the mouth. Two large serpent fangs usually appeared from his mouth. He always wore outsize ear ornaments and usually had a hat with several points that stood for the mountains in which he stored water.

CHAC, THE MAYA RAIN GOD

The Maya rain god Chac shared many characteristics with the Aztec Tláloc. It is thought the 'two' gods had a common ancestor in Olmec religion and even earlier worship.

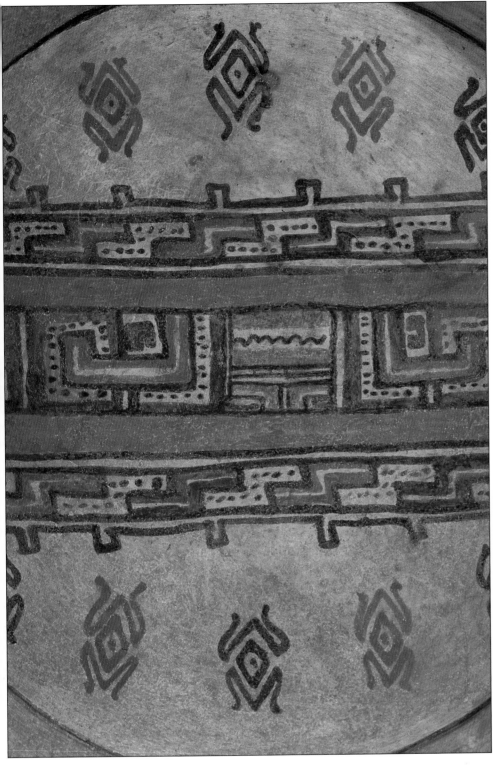

Left: Stylized forms of toads flank an abstract image of the rain god Chac on a terracotta plate found at Tikal.

in the Maya pantheon. Kings often wore the rain-god's mask in the Classic Period. The Hauberg stela of AD199, the earliest surviving artefact to bear writing in the Maya system, depicts a king wearing the mask of Chac.

THE RAIN GOD'S HELPERS

The rain god's helpers, the *chacs*, were assigned one to each of the four cardinal points. They are often depicted in Maya codices pouring out the waters of life from heavy vessels. Among the Yucatec Maya *chacs* were considered to be old men.

The *chacs* were also gods of thunder and stone axes were believed to be their thunderbolts. As among the Aztecs, worshippers burned copal resin incense – called *pom* by the Maya – to create black clouds of smoke that they believed had the power to call forth the larger rain-bearing black clouds in the sky.

Like Tláloc, Chac was god of lightning and mountain streams as well as of rains, and had helpers (called the *chacs* by the Maya) to assist him in his work. Chac was shown with a long nose, like a spout for pouring rainwater over the thirsty earth. He often had T-shaped eyes, representing rain falling from the sky. A remarkable homage to Chac was carved at Kabah (near Uxmal), where the building known as the Temple of the Masks is covered along its 50m- (150ft-) length with long-snouted faces of the rain god. The worship of the rain god was popular everywhere among the Maya. At Chichén Itzá, many offerings thrown into the sacred well (*cenote*) were made to Chac. The god is probably the most frequently represented

Right: Tláloc images characteristically have protruding fangs. This squat green stone vessel dates from c.AD200.

RAIN SUN AND WATER SUN

In one version of the Aztec creation story, the rain god Tláloc and his consort Chalchiúhtlicue were created by White Tezcatlipoca (Quetzalcóatl) and by Blue Tezcatlipoca (Huitzilopochtli) from parts of the body of the Earth Monster. Other parts were used to create the sky and earth. Tláloc then presided over the third sun or world age, the 'Rain Sun' (*Nahui Quiahuitl*). Chalchiúhtlicue was in charge of the fourth age, the 'Water Sun' (*Nahui Atl*). Tláloc also presided over one of the Aztec heavens: Tlalocán, a place of bliss where drought was not known, where waters and foods were plentiful and cocoa drinks could be made and enjoyed at leisure.

GODDESS OF THE WATERS

The goddess Chalchiúhtlicue was the deity of lakes, the ocean, rivers and streams. She was often represented wearing green or blue-and-white clothes

Left: This vast statue of water goddess Chalchiúhtlicue dates from c. AD150–450, the era of Teotihuacán.

and a hairband or crown of blue reeds. She was usually said to be Tláloc's wife, but was sometimes identified as his daughter or sister.

Chalchiúhtlicue was hailed as 'Mistress of the Jade Skirt' and 'Lady of the Lakes and Ocean' and sometimes wore seashells on her blue dresses. A necklace made of precious stones – usually jade beads – adorned her neck and she often wore either a delicate mosaic of turquoise over her ears or circular earrings. She also often wore a turquoise nose-ring. The Aztecs associated turquoise with the sky and the ocean and so held it particularly sacred to Tláloc and Chalchiúhtlicue. Members of the Aztec *pipiltin* (nobility) wore turquoise ornaments to signal their devotion to Tláloc and his consort.

Chalchiúhtlicue's connection to the expanses of water made her the patron goddess of fishermen and of water-carriers. Many Aztec images of Tláloc were carved of green jadeite, which the Aztecs called *chalchiuitl*.

Images of Chalchiúhtlicue sometimes represent her as a frog, a creature sacred to and specially protected by Tláloc. On the rain god's festival day, priests would leap into Lake Texcoco, calling and kicking like frogs.

More commonly, Tláloc's impersonator-priests would wear his easily recognizable mask, with goggle eyes, an upper lip ornament and fanged mouth, and sport a fine headdress of heron feathers.

Left: This Tláloc pot was deposited as an offering to the rain god facing his temple in Tenochtitlán.

They would carry a stalk of corn or a rod to symbolize the lightning that the rain god also controlled. In the mountains, where he was known to store his rain-waters, he could be seen in the form of tall-standing boulders. Tláloc's helpers, the *tláloques*, were sometimes said to be the rain god's children by his emerald consort. After Tláloc and the *tláloques* had done their work in the rainy season, the streams controlled by the water goddess rose. Precious water rushed between narrow banks in torrents that made the bare river beds of the dry season a distant memory. Chalchiúhtlicue was also associated with racing streams and whirlpools and was sometimes called 'The Foaming One'. She was represented sitting on a regal throne with water gushing forth about her.

SACRIFICE OF FROGS

In some accounts, Chalchiúhtlicue also had power over strong winds. Out of a clear sky she could summon hurricanes and whirlwinds with a destructive power to equal that of any flash flood. Like Tláloc, the goddess was associated with the fertility of the land, which was facilitated by the waters she controlled. She was also one of the goddesses of the maize plant. In her honour, a frog was sacrificed during the festival of the maize goddess Chicomecóatl. The creature was cooked and placed with a cornstalk and some ground maize before images of the maize goddess to represent the free-flowing waters that were so necessary if the maize was to flourish.

Chalchiúhtlicue's shrines were built alongside streams, rivers and lakes. Her most important place of worship was at Pantitlán, a spot in the middle of Lake Texcoco marked by banners, where a young woman or girl impersonating the goddess was sacrificed during the festival of Huey Tozoztli ('Major Vigil') in the fourth Aztec month (15 April–4 May). The goddess's links to fertility are made clear by this celebration. A tree named Tota ('Father') was carried to Pantitlán on a raft and set up at that spot to symbolize new life and regeneration in the fields surrounding the lake. The 'precious

Below: The bulk of this Tláloc statue, found in Mexico City, is suggestive of the awesome power of the storms he controls.

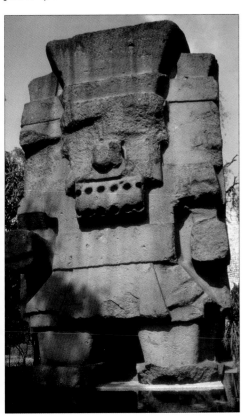

water' of the sacrificial victim's blood was then poured on to the surface of the lake, which the Aztecs hailed as Tonanhueyatl ('Mother Vast Water').

Chalchiúhtlicue was envisaged as a beautiful young woman, symbolizing the purity of the water in springs and fast-flowing streams or rivers. Her priestess took the central role in rites that early Spanish missionaries likened to Christian baptism for, among the Aztecs, new parents would take their baby to the priestess of Chalchiúhtlicue, who sprinkled the infant with spring water and dedicated him or her to the goddess.

SACRED ANIMALS
According to some accounts, during the celebration of the festival of Atlcahualo ('The Ending of Water') Tláloc's priests leapt into the waters of Lake Texcoco imitating the movements and calls of the frog, a creature sacred to Tláloc and Chalchiúhtlicue.

Above: In an image from the Codex Borbonicus, *Tláloc unleashes the rainwaters that the farmers long for.*

The duck was also a holy form of Tláloc. Like Tláloc, it can fly, swim and walk on land, is at home in the air (where Tláloc has power over rains and winds), in the water (where the rain god controls streams, rivers, lakes and oceans through his female counterpart Chalchiúhtlicue) and in the earth (where the rain god's fertilizing waters awaken the life held in the seeds of plants and make possible the germination of life).

Nappatecuhtli was a god associated with Tláloc and Chalchiúhtlicue. He was lord and patron of the respected craftsmen who made mats and thrones from reeds. Nappatecuhtli was depicted wearing a tall headdress decorated with quetzal feathers and strips of bark paper. He was shown holding a reed stick in one hand and a snake sceptre in the other.

THE FLAYED LORD

Above: Moctezuma receives ambassadors under the watchful eye of a Xipe Totec priest wearing a victim's flayed skin.

Like Tláloc, the Aztec god of vegetation and seeds, Xipe Totec, was an ancient deity whose worship was inherited by the Aztecs from earlier Mesoamericans. He was revered by the Zapotec builders of Monte Albán, where images of 'The Flayed Lord' have been found in tombs, and was also worshipped at Teotihuacán.

In Aztec belief, Xipe Totec was one of the four primary gods who were born from the union of Ometecuhtli and Omecíhuatl before the dawn of time. He was the oldest of the four, revered as Red Tezcatlipoca and associated with the east, where the new sun rises. He was the god of new shoots in spring and of the first growth of the maize plant.

FLAYING OF THE MEN

Xipe Totec was honoured with some distinctive and gruesome rites during the Tlacaxipehualiztli festival ('Flaying of the Men'), which was held in the second month of the Aztec year (6–25 March). This marked the start of the agricultural season, when seeds were germinating.

Sacrificial victims to Xipe Totec were shot to death with arrows so that the flow of their blood could symbolically represent the flow of rain on to the fields to nourish the seeds. At the festival's beginning, prisoners of war dressed as Xipe Totec were tied to a sacrificial stone and forced to defend themselves with mock weapons against fully armed warriors. After their death, the victims were flayed from head to toe. Priests then wore the skins over their own bodies for the entire month. Many sculptures of Xipe Totec show him wearing a flayed skin, drawn over his face and body and stitched up at the back. The mask of skin over the face usually allows the mouth and eyes of the wearer to show through.

This gruesome practice was a symbolic celebration of the splitting of seeds in the earth, which is a necessary part of their germination. The essence of plant life within the seed was likened to the essence of Xipe Totec in the sacrificial skin. The rite offered life to the gods to celebrate the renewal of life. Flaying may also have been practised on animals, for archaeologists have found statues of a coyote and a jaguar with their skin flayed along the backbone.

At the end of the festival, the priests divested themselves of the skins and stored them in a chamber within the sacred precinct in Tenochtitlán. For this purpose they used fired-clay bowls decorated with bobbles to suggest the puckered appearance of flayed skin. The bowls had tight-fitting lids to contain the smell of the rotting flesh.

Right: This image, found in an offering to Xipe Totec at Tepeji el Viejo, represents a priest wearing a flayed skin.

Above: An illustration from Bernardino de Sahagún's Florentine Codex *shows an Aztec planting the staple food maize.*

the animals were strong and broke away, each leaving part of its tail in the Twins' hands. For this reason those creatures have little or no tail. The only creature the boys did manage to corner was the rat. They caught him in a net and burned him over a fire to make him talk; ever afterwards the rat had no hairs on its tail.

The rat told the Twins that the field-clearing and farming techniques they had pioneered were not for them to develop and that they had a different destiny. They must follow the twin maize gods One Hunahpú and Seven Hunahpú to the underworld and tame the lords of that dark place. Some scholars believe this narrative to be a dramatization of the necessary move from a purely hunting lifestyle to a form of subsistence that relied both on hunting and domesticated food plants grown in laboriously cleared jungle fields.

CENTÉOTL AND DOMESTICATED MAIZE

The Aztecs had two main versions of the myth that described the discovery and first use of the domesticated maize plant. In one account the Plumed Serpent, Quetzalcóatl, transformed himself into an ant and brought the foodstuff back from the heart of 'food mountain', but in the variant myth the maize god Centéotl was the source of the staple food. The myth described how in the first years of the current world age Piltzintecuhtli, the son of the original human couple Oxomoco and Cipactonal, lived in great happiness with his beautiful wife Xochiquetzal. They had a son, who was named Centéotl. He was of earthy complexion and had ruddy good looks, full of the energy of the land. But despite his apparent good health Centéotl died suddenly and inexplicably – just as winter shrouds the land in lifeless cold. Then Piltzintecuhtli found no comfort in the beauty of his wife Xochiquetzal. He mourned his son long and loudly.

The gods themselves came down from the thirteen heavens and visited the grave of this fine young man. By their great goodness they caused his body to give issue to foods and useful plants, as the earth pushes up plants in spring: maize came from his fingernails and the sweet potato from his fingers, while cotton grew from his hair and other plants of great usefulness sprang from his body. And afterwards Centéotl was one of the many gods of maize revered by the Aztecs. In some versions of the myth Centéotl was the son of the Mesoamerican earth mother. She was known by the names of Teteoinnan or Tocitzin. In yet another account, he and flower goddess Xochiquetzal were the two children of Tlazoltéotl, goddess of childbirth, lust and dirt. Centéotl was also linked to Xochipilli, the flower god; both were strong young men with an abundance of creative energy.

Left: A Zapotec funerary urn, found at Monte Albán, honours the maize god.

SEX, PREGNANCY AND BIRTH

The flower goddess Xochiquetzal was patron of love and lovemaking, and she was also strongly associated with pregnancy and childbirth. According to one myth, she performed the first act of sexual congress, and in another account she was the first woman to give birth to twins.

Xochiquetzal was the archetype of youthful femininity, a young woman of great beauty and voluptuousness, with plentiful sexual allure. Her followers took the form of birds and butterflies. She was also embodied on earth in the first woman, who was fashioned from her hair in order to marry Piltzintecuhtli, the son of the primal couple Oxomoco and Cipactonal. The first woman took the goddess's name and had a son with Piltzintecuhtli named Centéotl, who after his death gave issue to the maize plant and was honoured as the maize god.

Xochiquetzal was the patron goddess of prostitutes. She protected the *ahuianime*, the city prostitutes, and the *maqui*, the priestess-prostitutes who attended to young single warriors and accompanied the soldiers on to the battlefield, where they willingly gave their lives. In some accounts, Xochiquetzal was the first woman to be sacrificed in battle. Her image in the *Codex Cospi* shows her in battle array, carrying a shield and arrows and wearing a warband as well as a garland of corn flowers.

The beautiful goddess enriched the world of men and women by giving flowers to grow on the side of the roadway and the steep mountain paths. These flowers were made from her vulva. In one myth

Below: This Olmec terracotta figure of a baby is from the dawn of Mesoamerican culture.

she was wife to Quetzalcóatl or the Plumed Serpent. One day as he was washing himself he allowed his hands to move over his penis and the seeds that spilled forth became the first bat. The gods sent this creature to visit the bountiful Xochiquetzal. It bit the goddess in her vulva and carried a piece of flesh away to the other gods. They made roses from the bat's gift, but these flowers did not smell good. The bat repeated his visit to Xochiquetzal and this time took the flesh to Mictlantecuhtli, the lord of the underworld. This time the roses were as sweet-smelling and beautiful as anyone could wish. These marvellous flowers were the gift of the goddess Xochiquetzal to the peoples of the world.

TLAZOLTÉOTL

The form of the mother-fertility goddess most powerfully connected to childbirth was Tlazoltéotl, the goddess of filth, excrement and sexual lust. She was often depicted squatting in the position that Mesoamerican women usually adopted for childbirth. Tlazoltéotl was associated with penitential rites, including the

Left: Tlazoltéotl, squatting in the typical Mesoamerican childbirth position, is a goddess of opposites, associated both with the noise of lust and the quiet of penitence. The image is from the Codex Vaticanus.

confession of sins. In one myth she was also a great temptress, who used her sexual power to unpick the virtue of a pious man.

This man was determined to win the gods' favour and took himself away from family life to settle on a rocky promontory in the northern desert. The gods wanted to probe the man's commitment, so they despatched the demon Yáotl ('The Enemy'), a much-feared manifestation of Tezcatlipoca, to test him. Yáotl the seducer brought forth a parade of the world's most beautiful women who called up to the pilgrim and tried to tempt him down, if only for a short break from his demanding religious observance. Backwards and forwards they went on the rocky ground, calling up to him and seductively singing the latest songs from the brothels of Tenochtitlán. However, the man refused to look at them and turned back to his sacred rites.

Viewing this from afar, Tlazoltéotl was determined to join in. She came to that inhospitable windswept place dressed in her finest and most seductive outfit and called up sweetly to the man, asking

Below: Tlazoltéotl rides the snake of sexuality and a broom with which she sweeps away the sins of the sorrowful.

to be allowed to climb the rock for a conversation: perhaps she could learn something from him? Such was her appeal that he agreed to allow her to climb up. When she arrived there beside him she was to him as a breeze to a soldier in the desert, like a sweet and suddenly attainable dream to a man cursed by insomnia, and he succumbed to temptation.

Yáotl then appeared beside the couple and turned the man into a scorpion. Afterwards he fetched the man's wife and brought her to the place, told her the full story of her husband's disgrace and turned her into a scorpion

Above: A page from the Codex Mendoza *illustrates the rites and experiences that fill the first months of an Aztec baby's life.*

too. They lived on in the desert under a rock and produced many generations of scorpions.

Another Aztec goddess associated with childbirth was Chalchiúhtlicue, wife of Tláloc. She was a patron of newly born children and was believed to protect virtuous married couples and honourable loves. Among the Maya, the goddess Ix Chel, consort of the supreme god Itzamná, was considered to be a protectress of women in childbirth.

CHAPTER FIVE

AFTER DEATH

From his place at the summit of the thirteen Aztec heavens, the primeval being Ometeotl, lord of duality, sent forth the souls of human babies about to be born. Ometeotl lived in his dual forms as Ometecuhtli and Omecíhuatl in the twelfth and thirteenth layers of heaven, in a place called Omeyocán. Here also lived the souls of babies who had died before their time and without cause, and those who had died inexplicably in their sleep. They expected a new life in a world freshly made after the cataclysmic end of the fifth sun or world age in a great earthquake. In Omeyocán a fork of the cosmic tree provided sweet milk for the nourishment of these babies' souls and the spirits newly made by Ometeotl.

The duality embodied by Ometeotl informed every particle of the sacred Mesoamerican universe. For the Aztecs and Maya, darkness was everywhere balanced by its opposite, light, night by day, dampness by dryness, feminine by masculine, death by life, the shadowy underworld by the bright heavens. The cosmic tree that held the centre grew both in heaven and on the earth, both on the earth and in the underworld. The level of the flat earth or Tlalticpac was the first plane of the nine underworld realms and also the first plane of the thirteen celestial realms. It was both celestial and terrestrial and also both terrestrial and infernal. Everywhere, two was also one: so darkness and light were both one and differentiated. Nothing was purely good or bad, for the good lay within the bad and vice versa; the gods possessed duality and had positive and negative attributes.

Left: The nine levels of the Temple of the Inscriptions at Palenque symbolize the nine levels of the underworld.

THE PARADISE OF THE FLOWER GODDESS

Tamoanchán, the level of the thirteen Aztec heavens presided over by the beautiful flower goddess Xochiquetzal, was imagined as an earthly paradise. There the branches of the cosmic tree were heavily laden with blossoms and fruit and released sweet perfume into the sunlit air. In some accounts, Tamoanchán was literally an earthly place, hidden near the holy peak of a mythical mountain in the far, far south, the region of Huitzilopochtli, where the air was thin and delightfully cool and the rocks rose almost to the moon herself. However, it was usually said to be high above the earth where the heavens climbed to a different sphere of reality.

RAW MATERIAL FOR HUMAN CREATION

Quetzalcóatl and Xólotl brought the bones they rescued from the underworld to Tamoanchán at the start of the fifth world age. In this fertile paradise they

Below: An Aztec relief carving shows four-toothed Tláloc with the skulls of people whose death has given them access to his heaven.

presented the raw material for a new human creation to the other gods. The deities gathered in the sweet air of the flower goddess's paradise to provide blood to mix with the ground bones and so make a paste with which to form the first boy and girl. These first humans were nurtured in Tamoanchán, but the human race would never be permitted to return to that place. It was an abode of the gods.

FALL OF THE GODDESS

Meanwhile in Tamoanchán, Xochiquetzal passed her time weaving wonderful textiles in inspirational colours and patterns. She had many loyal maidens to keep her company and from time to time they would pause in their work to laugh at the antics of entertainers. Tamoanchán was a happy home for the goddess but, according to one of the myths, Xochiquetzal was thrown out of the restful paradise and made to spend the full expanse of time on the Earth.

According to this tale, the fruits and blossom on the tree that perfumed Tamoanchán were sweet and tempting to anyone curious, whether divine or human. The creator lord Ometeotl had decreed that this tree should not be touched. It was permitted, however, for the birds of Tamoanchán to alight on its branches and fill them with sweet song and for other animals to scamper up the trunk and leap hither and thither, but the gods and goddesses must not taste the fruits or pick the flowers.

Left: Heavenly flower goddess Xochiquetzal was associated with nose-rings shaped like a butterfly.

Xochiquetzal was captivated by the tree's beauty, which balanced and mirrored her own. Temptation got the better of her on a day when heady delight drove her from her sense of what is right. She picked a garland of flowers for her perfumed hair and stole and tasted one of the ripe red fruits of the tree. She thought that no one would know. What could be the harm, when the tree had so many blossoms, fruits and flowers on its heavy branches? However, in the instant that she violated the supreme lord's command, the tree began to shudder and then cracked and fell into two great pieces, just like the tree made from the entwined bodies of Quetzalcóatl and Mayáhuel in another place. Blood oozed from the spot where she had plucked the fruit and from the place where the two halves had split.

Restrained in his anger but determined to uphold the sanctity of his commands, Ometeotl told Xochiquetzal of her fate. She would be sent down to the mountains and dry plains of earth and live in that place, mourning her loss. She would weep as she passed and touched the flowers and blossoms and she would henceforth be known as Ixnextli ('Ash Eyes'). Xochiquetzal's enjoyment of beauty, of the flowers that she gave to men and women, would be limited because her vision would be blurred by ever-flowing tears.

Left: Xochipilli and Xochiquetzal are usually considered brother and sister. Xochiquetzal is often shown with quetzal feathers in her headdress.

PASSAGE TO THE HEAVENS

According to the Aztecs, only the souls of those who died in particular ways found passage to the heavens. The spirits of warriors who died in the heat of battle – a dart piercing their neck, their last breath escaping in desperation – would wake in the heaven presided over by Tonatiuh, an aspect of the sun god.

They were joined in this blessed place by the souls of women who died during or after desperate labours, their infant warrior-sons having – like Huitzilopochtli – delivered death at the beginning of life. Tonatiuh's heaven was called Ilhuicatl Tonatiuh ('Sun Heaven') or Tonatiuichan. The souls of sacrificial victims also passed after death to Tonatiuh's heaven.

The souls of those who drowned in a sudden flood or when a canoe capsized, the souls of unfortunates who had been stricken by illnesses associated with water, and the souls of people caught in a violent storm or struck by lightning would find themselves in Tláloc's heaven, Tlalocán. This was a realm blessed with the utmost fertility, a land where water gently touched the brow in a light, warm drizzle that pleased the plants and encouraged them to deliver cacao beans and the finest fruits in abundance.

Below: This wall painting at Teotihuacán may represent inhabitants of Tlalocán, the paradise of the rain god.

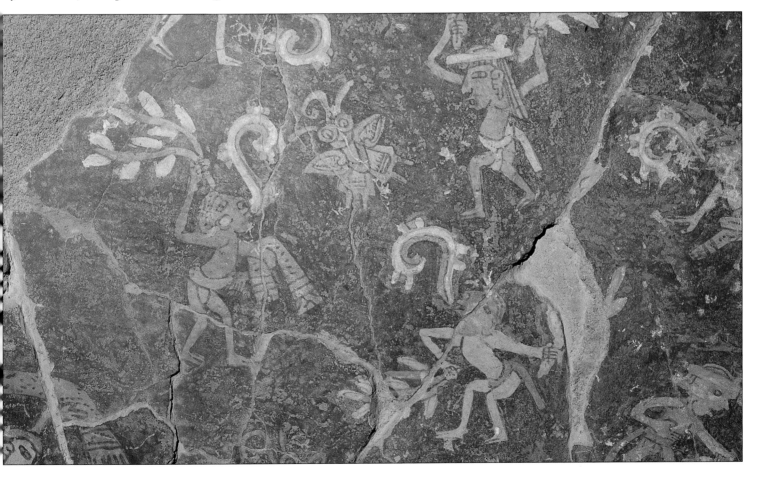

THE BACABS AND THE COSMIC TREE

Like the Aztecs, the Maya also believed that in the centre of the universe the world tree linked the heavens, the earth and the underworld. According to one tradition of Maya cosmology, four giants named the bacabs, the sons of the supreme lord Itzamná and his goddess Ix Chel, upheld the four corners of the world in the north, south, east and west. The splendid sarcophagus of King Pacal at Palenque depicts the king's spirit making the journey downwards from the terrestrial level to the underworld along the length of the world tree.

ACCESS TO SPIRIT REALMS

The world tree could also serve as a conduit for spirits to access the realms above and below during this life. It delivered worshippers to a paradise of ecstatic spiritual experience through shamanistic voyaging. In this guise, the tree might be associated with the Vision Serpent. The Maya summoned the Vision Serpent during the solemn rites of autosacrifice

Below: This three-faced Maya brazier is from the Postclassic Period. Psychedelic substances powered Maya spirit journeys.

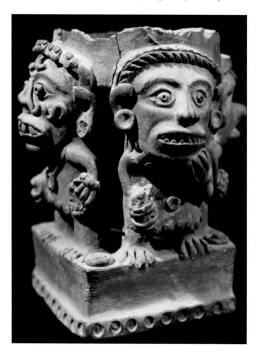

in which worshippers cut themselves and offered the blood of their own wounds to the gods. The intricate carvings of Lady Xoc, wife of Shield Jaguar, at Yaxchilán, show her gaining access to a heightened state brought on by rites of bloodletting to the Vision Serpent. Through the jaws of the Serpent she connects to the sacred ancestors and the gods.

The psychedelic mushroom *Psilocybe aztecorum* also provided access to spirit realms and may sometimes have been identified with the world tree. A striking ceramic discovered at Colima, in Mexico, depicts religious celebrants dancing around a central column with an umbrella-like top, which apparently represented either the world tree or the mushroom.

Maya priests and worshippers took the *Psilocybe aztecorum* mushroom to induce a religious trance. Throughout the Maya region, archaeologists have discovered stone effigies of mushrooms set up in the period 1000BC–AD500. It was highly valued – and perhaps even worshipped – alongside tobacco flowers and morning glory flowers, for its hallucinogenic properties. Scholars believe that the Maya gained their knowledge of the bright celestial realms and of the dark underworld in the course of spirit journeys brought about through the use of psychedelic substances. Paintings on Classic Period Maya ceramics reveal that Maya nobles and priests took ritual enemas of liquids containing the peyote cactus to bring on visions.

A LUXURIOUS AFTERLIFE

Some Maya traditions held that a few lucky souls would be admitted to a heavenly realm rather similar to the Tamoanchán of the Aztecs. There they would not need to perform backbreaking work cutting terraced fields from mountainsides or thick jungle, but could rest from the hunt or the long trading journeys they had made in their lifetimes

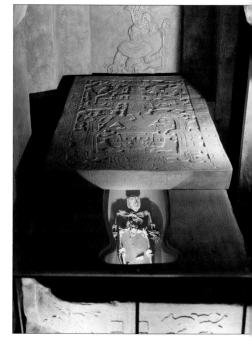

Above: A stone depicts King Pacal's journey to the underworld in this reconstruction of his crypt at Palenque.

and simply find luxury all about them. They could lie in the sweet shade provided by the cosmic tree. When they were thirsty they could gather some cacao beans, to make chocolate drink.

THE WAY TO PARADISE THROUGH THE UNDERWORLD

Most souls were destined for the underworld. Mythical narratives such as the account in the Quiché Maya *Popol Vuh* of the Hero Twins' descent to the underworld dramatized the many tests that the spirit would have to go through there. The *Popol Vuh* tale and the Classic Period myths on which it was based were a kind of guidebook to the afterlife.

The Hero Twins' narrative ends with Hunahpú and Xbalanqué defeating death in the form of the underworld lords and rising triumphant to the heavens. It was generally understood that their triumph in the underworld paved the way for those who came after them. A tablet at Palenque shows a ruler emerging from

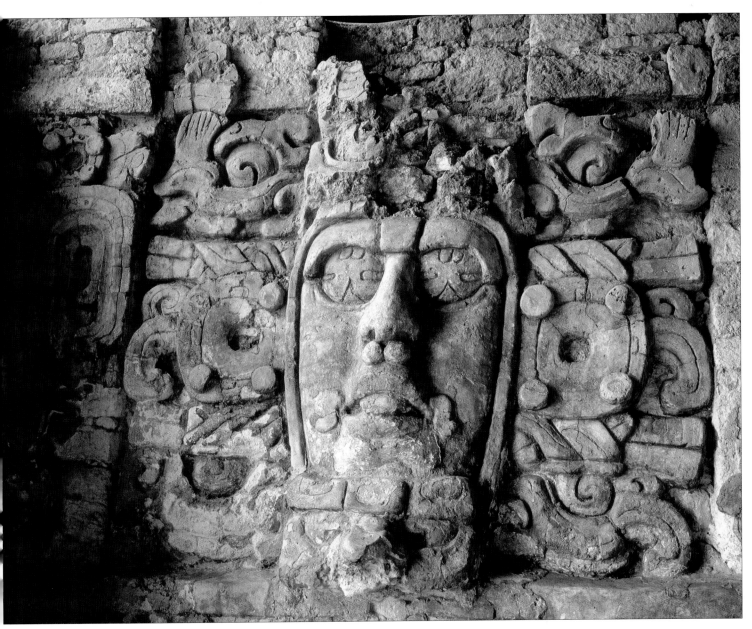

Above: This mask of the sun god is from an Early Classic Maya pyramid at Kohunlich, Quintana Roo.

the underworld in the appearance of the jaguar god of that realm and being greeted with an offering by his mother. Death could not hold him and that cold ogre could not expect to contain any of the ruler's descendants.

According to some scholars, the Maya believed that only the noble elite would proceed to an afterlife by way of the tests in the underworld. Other authorities argue such a religion would not have been generally sustainable and that people at all levels of society must have believed that their ancestors had somehow triumphed over death and that they themselves might do the same.

In its celebration of new life out of death the story informs a splendid late Classic Period tripod plate (*c.*AD600–900) that depicts the father of the Hero Twins' One Hunahpú being born from the cracked back of a great turtle.

According to the version given in the *Popol Vuh*, One Hunahpú is unable to leave the underworld. On this plate, however, and perhaps also in the Classic Period version of the myth, he is given new

life by his sons. The Maya saw the turtle as an image of the earth and identified One Hunahpú as the Young Maize God, so the image on the plate emphasizes the myth's meaning as a celebration of the life-cycle of the maize plant. However, the plate is also a truly joyful celebration of the defeat of darkness and death and of the spirit's rebirth into light and life.

Left: A clay censer found in Yucatán bears the face of a little known Maya deity who was patron of bee-keepers.

THE JOURNEY TO MICTLÁN

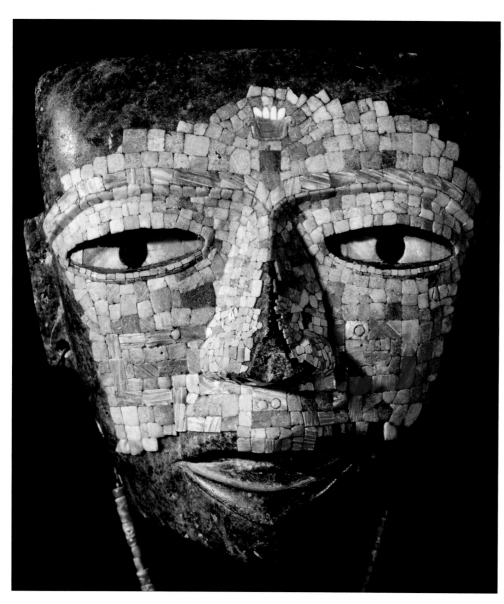

one's consciousness lived; and the liver, home to the spirit. The liver was associated with Mictlán, realm of the spirits, by ancient Aztec tradition. Mictlantecuhtli wore sandals as a sign of his lordly standing. His consort, Mictecacíhuatl, had a fearsome skull for her face, and her thin breasts sagged despairingly. Her skirt was made of flailing fork-tongued serpents.

The underworld was the particular realm of dogs. Mictlantecuhtli was patron of the day *itzcuintli* ('dog'). Dogs were often sacrificed on their master's death and laid in his tomb, for the animals were expected to guide their masters through the ordeal after death. An underworld dog appeared to help new arrivals across the first hazard they faced.

The dead were buried with equipment to help them on their journey. They were given gifts for Mictlantecuhtli and Mictecacíhuatl, as well as paper clothes, food, water, blankets and a jade bead to serve as a replacement heart.

Below: With saucer eyes and terrible teeth, Mictecacíhuatl makes a suitably grim consort for the lord of the underworld.

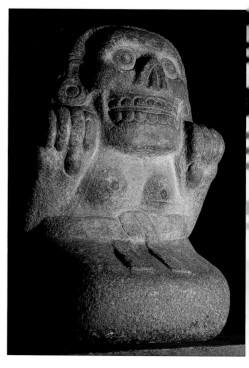

In the Aztec underworld, the god Mictlantecuhtli enjoyed his power in dampness and darkness. Everything in the universe had its balancing double, the other half of a perfect duality. Mictlantecuhtli and his consort Mictecacíhuatl were the underworld equivalents of Ometecuhtli and Omecíhuatl in the uppermost layers of the Aztec heaven.

Above: This jade, coral, obsidian and turquoise mosaic mask is a funerary ornament from Texmilincan, Mexico.

THE UNDERWORLD GOD
The underworld god was skeletal because he had lost half his flesh, and his black curly hair sparkled with stars. He was often depicted dressed in clothes made from strips of bark paper. He had enormous, clawlike hands capable of tearing the underworld spirits limb from limb and was happy to see others suffer.

Mictlantecuhtli was essentially a personification of death. His liver hung from a gaping hole in his stomach. The Aztecs believed that the body had three principal parts: the head, where a person's destiny was housed; the heart, where

TESTING THE DEAD

The soul had to negotiate different hazards at each of the nine levels of the underworld. The first was to find a way over a raging river torrent. Here a yellow or red dog appeared as a guide. The second test was to pass between towering mountains that would suddenly and terrifyingly crash together, with the noise of countless jaguars roaring as if preparing to rip flesh from bone.

The pilgrim went on through a demanding range of tests. He had to climb a mountain made of dark obsidian, the shadowy 'smoking' glass worn by the dark lord Tezcatlipoca, then survive an icy northern wind cold enough to peel the skin from the cheeks of a living man. Next he had to defeat a ravening snake, then a dread alligator, before crossing eight deserts and climbing eight great mountains. Exhaustion threatened the

Below: A gruesome Mixtec drinking cup from Zaachila, Mexico, is intended to remind drinkers of their mortality.

poor spirit, but then came a biting wind to drive him on. This gale was filled with knives of obsidian, the blades so sharp that they could slice through solid rock as easily as cut up a tortilla. Next he faced a demon named Izpuzteque, with dreadful backwards-facing legs, and then another foe who tried to blind the spirit traveller by throwing handfuls of ash in his eyes. Finally, he came face to face with Mictlantecuhtli and Mictecacíhuatl and made offerings to them. Mictlantecuhtli would rip the poor pilgrim's spirit-body to pieces. This did not end the soul's existence, for he lived on in the domain of Mictlantecuhtli and Mictecacíhuatl, in dampness and darkness, with only his companions and friends among those who had died before him to give him any pleasure or comfort. However, once a year he was permitted to return to the lands of living Mesoamerica, where his relatives would lay out earthly foods for his pleasure.

Sometimes the Aztecs located Mictlán in the far north, a desolate, dry place of dreadful famines and cold winds, associated with the colours yellow and black, with the sacrificial knife and with the dark lord Tezcatlipoca. A realm of endless fear and ill-fortune, it was the northern pole balancing the mountaintop heaven situated in the far south. It was known as Mictlampa ('Abode of the Dead'), or as Tlalxicco ('Earth's Navel'). More usually it was understood to be below the earth.

Mictlán was the place where the gods stored the bones of past generations, both from this age and from previous eras. At the beginning of the current world age, Quetzalcóatl visited the underworld in the company of his dog aspect Xólotl to gather these bones in order to fashion the first people. The Aztecs' understanding of duality meant that death always included life and

Above: Mictlantecuhtli, sunken-cheeked and horribly grimacing, keeps watch over the cold, famine-ravaged realm of the dead.

new beginnings. The seeds of future creation lay in the underworld, just as the seeds of future plants could be buried unseen in the earth. For this reason, skull masks used in religious rites and placed as offerings usually had bright shining eyes. These masks are usually now missing their eyes because the precious materials used have been stripped by the conquistadors or other gold diggers.

BEYOND THE WATER

The Maya underworld was ruled by the lords One Death and Seven Death. Its inhabitants roamed the underground kingdom desperately, their bodies disintegrating as they went. Images of Xibalba in codices and on Classic Period vases show spirit forms with horribly distended bellies and eyes hanging on cords from their sockets. Like Mictlantecuhtli, they found their flesh falling from their bones, allowing their stomach, liver and other organs to tumble out hideously. They could not control their bodily functions and streams of excrement and wind burst out. Some wore necklaces made from the fallen eyeballs of other poor souls.

LORDS OF THE UNDERWORLD

According to the account in the *Popol Vuh*, the Maya underworld lords had blood-chilling names and specialities. Jaundice Demon was master of that disease and climbed to earth to make people sicken, while Pus Demon followed in his footsteps and would cause people's limbs to swell and poison to seep from their bandaged wounds.

Below: This monstrous serpent appears on a late Classic Period Maya drinking cup from Motagua Valley, Guatemala.

Above: Bats were frequent tormentors of the spirit traveller in the Maya 'Place of Fright'. This urn was made in the Toltec period.

Two other lords were Bone Sceptre and Skull Sceptre, who carried bare human bones as staffs of authority and brought wasting diseases in their train; illnesses that caused the flesh to fall away until sufferers were good for nothing but a lonely death.

House Corner and Blood Gatherer were hungry for blood, like vampire bats or leeches. Humans could not relax in their presence, for they would come out of the shadows with their sharp teeth bared to assault the soft neck and other vulnerable parts of a man or woman's body.

The Lord of Rubbish and the Stabbing Lord were found in places where people had left remains of their meals or other activities lying around the homes. These dark gods would attack from the blind side and bring their victims low with sharp stabbing pains and fierce strikes. Packstrap and Wing trailed the roads like the Aztec god Tezcatlipoca, seeking the

unwary. When they struck they caused sudden death. The victim's mouth would flood and bright blood would run on to his chin, stain his chest and gush on to the ground when he collapsed. The victim would die in the roadway, alone like a diseased dog, with the dark wind blowing desolately past.

The aged god Pauahtun, one of many patron gods of scribes, was also strongly associated with the underworld. His old and sunken face surrounded a gap-toothed mouth and Pauahtun also wore a net head-wrapping in which the tools of his scribal arts sometimes appear. According to one tradition, Pauahtun supported the weight of the earth above him and so he was from time to time depicted with one hand above his head.

CHAPTER SIX

MYTHS AND HISTORY

Mesoamericans created narratives not only about the world's beginnings and the deeds of the gods, but also about the origins of their own people and the history of the tribe. Indeed the Aztecs and other Mesoamericans often took a creative approach to history, blending fact and narratives of the past in a way designed to establish political and religious points in the present.

According to an origin narrative shared by the Aztecs and many of their neighbours, the earliest human ancestors emerged from a collection of sacred caverns known as Chicomoztoc ('Seven Caves'). The Aztecs believed that the seven womb-like caves radiated out from a central chamber and that one people or tribe emerged from each cave.

Chicomoztoc was generally understood to be in the north and was associated with dryness, darkness, barrenness and lack of civilization; it was a good place to leave behind. Several attempts have been made to identify both this place of origin and the place known as Aztlán ('Land of the Cranes') from which the Aztecs claimed to have started out when they made a southward pilgrimage to the Valley of Mexico. The story appears to express the tribes' feeling that they were born from and belong to the mother goddess. However, some historians suggest that the myth is symbolic of the transition from a nomadic hunting lifestyle to a more settled lifestyle of farming supplemented by hunting; a change that equated to a rebirth and gave the former nomads a new connection to the land.

Left: This Codex Durán *image depicts Moctezuma leaving on a retreat after hearing of the Spanish landing.*

TOLTEC WANDERINGS

The Toltecs, so revered by the Aztecs as the builders of the wondrous city of Tollán, were probably the first of many tribes who travelled southward from the wasteland of the north, beginning as nomads but settling in the more fertile lands further south and learning the skills of settled life. According to one account given by the chronicler Fernando de Alva Ixtlilxóchitl, the Toltecs came south by sea, following the coastline presumably in large sea-going Mesoamerican canoes, until they came to the mythical land of Tlapallán ('Land of Bright Colours'). Scholars regard this version of events as highly unlikely, preferring a more probable land route, but they do note that in some traditions the god Quetzalcóatl was regarded as an expert in navigating a canoe and that on the eastern edge of Mesoamerica Maya traders proved themselves capable of covering large distances by sea canoe.

DISPLACEMENT OF A PEOPLE

The Toltecs began their journey because they were displaced by a stronger, better-equipped or more warlike people, setting the pattern for generations of brief

Below: The Aztecs looked back to the Toltecs with the awe they felt for the grave offerings of Teotihuacán. This stone mask was placed on the face of a buried Teotihuacán noble.

Above: The Toltecs' travels to find a homeland lasted more than 100 years and included 13 brief periods of settlement.

settlements and enforced migrations. Ixtlilxóchitl's chronicle records that the Toltecs landed in Tlapallán in the year 1-Técpatl, identified by scholars as AD387. The chronicle then suggests that they were driven out from Tlapallán around 50 years later, in AD439, after rebelling against the king's authority. They settled nearby for eight years, then travelled to Tlapallantzinco, where they

rested for three years. Afterwards they began a long migration along the Pacific coast and across northern Mexico. According to Ixtlilxóchitl's chronicle, the Toltecs at last found the appointed place to establish their wondrous city of Tollán in AD566.

PICTURE ACKNOWLEDGEMENTS
The Art Archive: 9t, 59l, 65t, 66l, 76l, 81t and b, 82t, 84b, 90r, 102t, 108r, 117t, 124l, /Bodleian Library, Oxford: 85r, /Album/Joseph Martin: 18l, 110t, /Museo de America, Madrid: 63t, 104l, /Nicolas Sapieha: 36b, /Dagli Orti: 15t, 17t, 23b, 24t, 25b, 37l, 42t, 48t, 54bl, 60t and bl, 68r, 69b, 70r, 71t and r, 72l and r, 73t, 74r, 78t, 79l, 82l, 83r, 86–7, 90l, 91t and b, 92l, 94l and r, 95t and b, 96bl, 97t, 98t and r, 99l, 100t and l, 101l and r, 103l and r, 104r, 105b, 106–7, 109b, 110l, 112r, 113r, 114l and r, 115t and b, 116t and b, 117b, 118b, 119b, 120l and r, 121l, 123t, 124t, 125l and r, 126t, 127b, 128tl, /Eileen Tweedy: 19b, 102b, /Mireille Vautier: 15bl, 66–7, 75l, 77l and r, 80l, 89t, 105t, 111r and b, 112l, 122l, 123r, 128b.
The Bridgeman Art Library: 14l, 22t, 24b, 27b, 28b, 40l, 52l, 99l, /Brooklyn Museum of Art, New York: 54br, /Giraudon: 19tr, 22b, 69tl, /Ian Mursell/Mexicolore: 37t, 60br, /Banco Mexicano de Imagenes/ INAH: 16t, 35t, 38l, 43t, 48b, 50r, 53l and r, 59t, 61t, 64t, /Sean Sprague/Mexicolore: 46–7.
Corbis: /Archivo Iconografico, S.A.:, 30–1, 32, 34r, /Yann Arthus-Bertrand: 42b, /Bettmann: 85t, /Bettmann: 74l, /Historical Picture Archive: 68l, /Kimbell Art Museum: 27tr, /C. and J. Lenars:10t, 11t and b, 49t, Gianni Dagli Orti: 21b, 51, 56b, 63l.

Werner Forman: 34b, 61b, 89b, /Anthropology Museum, Veracruz University, Jalapa: 14l, 93r, /Biblioteca Universitaria, Bologna: 52r, /British Museum, London: 44b, 45b, 50l, 56t, 58r, 65l, 80t, 97r, 121r, /Philip Goldman, London: 70t, /Liverpool Museum, Liverpool: 12–13, 16b, 29t, 79t, 85r, /Edward H. Merrin Gallery, New York: 28t, /Museum of the Americas, New York: 11b, /Museum für Völkerkunde, Basle: 62r, 75r, 88r, /Museum für Völkerkunde, Berlin: 17b, 39b, /Museum für Völkerkunde, Hamburg: 39t, /National Museum of Anthropology, Mexico: 20t, 21t, 27tl, 38r, 44t, 45t, 57l and r, 62l, 88l, 92r, 93l, /National Museum of Denmark, Copenhagen: 20bl, /Pigorini Museum of Prehistory and Ethnography, Rome: 33t, /private collection, New York: 25t, 54t, 108l, /St Louis Art Museum, MO: 43b, /Smithsonian Institution, Washington: 40t, /Sotheby's, New York, 18t, /Dr Kurt Stavanenhagen Collection, Mexico City: 36t, 84t.
N.J. Saunders: 41b, 55.
South American Pictures/Tony Morrison: 7, 35b, 73l, /Chris Sharp: 8t, 26b, 58b, 109t, 113l.